First Grand Challenge and Workshop on Human Multimodal Language 2018

Held at ACL 2018

Melbourne, Australia
20 July 2018

ISBN: 978-1-5108-6720-8

ACL 2018

**First Grand Challenge and Workshop
on Human Multimodal Language (Challenge-HML)**

Proceedings of the Workshop

July 20, 2018
Melbourne, Australia

Introduction

Welcome to the First Grand Challenge and Workshop on Human Multimodal Language (Challenge-HML). This grand challenge is co-located with ACL 2018 in Melbourne, Australia. During this grand challenge, we aim to gauge the performance of current natural language processing models in understanding the complete form of human language: from language, vision and acoustic modalities all used in a coordinated manner to convey intentions.

Computational analysis of human multimodal language is an emerging research area in Natural Language Processing (NLP). It expands the horizons of NLP to study language used in face to face communication and in online multimedia. This form of language contains modalities of language (in terms of spoken text), visual (in terms of gestures and facial expressions) and acoustic (in terms of changes in the voice tone). At its core, this research area is focused on modeling the three modalities and their complex interactions. The first Grand Challenge and Workshop on Human Multimodal Language aims to facilitate the growth of this new research direction in NLP community. The grand challenge is focused on multimodal sentiment analysis and emotion recognition on the recently introduced CMU Multimodal Opinion Sentiment and Emotion Intensity (CMU-MOSEI) dataset. The grand-challenge will be held in conjunction with the 56th Annual Meeting of the Association for Computational Linguistics 2018.

Communicating using multimodal language (verbal and nonverbal) shares a significant portion of our communication including face-to-face communication, video chatting, and social multimedia opinion sharing. Hence, it's computational analysis is centric to NLP research. The challenges of modeling human multimodal language can be split into two major categories: 1) studying each modality individually and modeling each in a manner that can be linked to other modalities (also known as intramodal dynamics) 2) linking the modalities by modeling the interactions between them (also known as intermodal dynamics). Common forms of these interactions include complementary or correlated information across modes. Intrinsic to each modality, modeling human multimodal language is complex due to factors such as idiosyncrasy in communicative styles, non-trivial alignment between modalities and unreliable or contradictory information across modalities. Therefore computational analysis becomes a challenging research area.

Organizers:

Amir Zadeh Language Technologies Institute, Carnegie Mellon University
Louis-Philippe Morency Language Technologies Institute, Carnegie Mellon University
Paul Pu Liang Machine Learning Department, Carnegie Mellon University
Soujanya Poria Temasek Laboratories, Nanyang Technological University
Erik Cambria Temasek Laboratories, Nanyang Technological University
Stefan Scherer Institute for Creative Technologies, University of Southern California

Invited Speakers:

Bing Liu, University of Illinois at Chicago (UIC)
Sharon Oviatt, Monash University
Roland Goecke, University of Canberra

Table of Contents

Grand Challenge and Workshop Program

July 20th 2018

9:00–10:30   **Session 1**

9:00–9:10   *Opening Remarks*

9:10–10:00   *Keynote*
Bing Liu

10:00–10:10   *Getting the subtext without the text: Scalable multimodal sentiment classification from visual and acoustic modalities*
Nathaniel Blanchard, Daniel Moreira, Aparna Bharati and Walter Scheirer

10:10–10:20   *Recognizing Emotions in Video Using Multimodal DNN Feature Fusion*
Jennifer Williams, Steven Kleinegesse, Ramona Comanescu and Oana Radu

10:20–10:30   *Multimodal Relational Tensor Network for Sentiment and Emotion Classification*
Saurav Sahay, Shachi H Kumar, Rui Xia, Jonathan Huang and Lama Nachman

10:30–11:00   *Coffee Break*

11:00–12:30   **Session 2**

11:00–11:50   *Keynote*
Sharon Oviatt

11:50–12:00   *Advances in Multimodal Datasets*
Paul Pu Liang

12:00–12:10   *Convolutional Attention Networks for Multimodal Emotion Recognition from Speech and Text Data*
Woo Yong Choi, Kyu Ye Song and Chan Woo Lee

12:10–12:20   *Sentiment Analysis using Imperfect Views from Spoken Language and Acoustic Modalities*
Imran Sheikh, Sri Harsha Dumpala, Rupayan Chakraborty and Sunil Kumar Kopparapu

July 20th 2018 (continued)

12:20–12:30   *Polarity and Intensity: the Two Aspects of Sentiment Analysis*
Leimin Tian, Catherine Lai and Johanna Moore

12:30–13:30   *Lunch Break*

13:30–15:00   Session 3

13:30–14:20   *Keynote*
Roland Goecke

14:20–14:30   *ASR-based Features for Emotion Recognition: A Transfer Learning Approach*
Noé Tits, Kevin El Haddad and Thierry Dutoit

14:30–14:40   *Seq2Seq2Sentiment: Multimodal Sequence to Sequence Models for Sentiment Analysis*
Hai Pham, Thomas Manzini, Paul Pu Liang and Barnabas Poczos

14:40–14:50   *DNN Multimodal Fusion Techniques for Predicting Video Sentiment*
Jennifer Williams, Ramona Comanescu, Oana Radu and Leimin Tian

14:50–15:00   *Grand Challenge Results*

15:00   *Workshop End*

Getting the subtext without the text: Scalable multimodal sentiment classification from visual and acoustic modalities

Nathaniel Blanchard
Dept. of Comp. Sci. and Eng.
University of Notre Dame, USA
nblancha@nd.edu

Daniel Moreira
Dept. of Comp. Sci. and Eng.
University of Notre Dame, USA
dhenriq1@nd.edu

Aparna Bharati
Dept. of Comp. Sci. and Eng.
University of Notre Dame, USA
abharati@nd.edu

Walter J. Scheirer
Dept. of Comp. Sci. and Eng.
University of Notre Dame, USA
walter.scheirer@nd.edu

Abstract

In the last decade, video blogs (vlogs) have become an extremely popular method through which people express sentiment. The ubiquitousness of these videos has increased the importance of multimodal fusion models, which incorporate video and audio features with traditional text features for automatic sentiment detection. Multimodal fusion offers a unique opportunity to build models that learn from the full depth of expression available to human viewers. In the detection of sentiment in these videos, acoustic and video features provide clarity to otherwise ambiguous transcripts. In this paper, we present a multimodal fusion model that exclusively uses high-level video and audio features to analyze spoken sentences for sentiment. We discard traditional transcription features in order to minimize human intervention and to maximize the deployability of our model on at-scale real-world data. We select high-level features for our model that have been successful in non-affect domains in order to test their generalizability in the sentiment detection domain. We train and test our model on the newly released CMU Multimodal Opinion Sentiment and Emotion Intensity (CMU-MOSEI) dataset, obtaining an F_1 score of 0.8049 on the validation set and an F_1 score of 0.6325 on the held-out challenge test set.

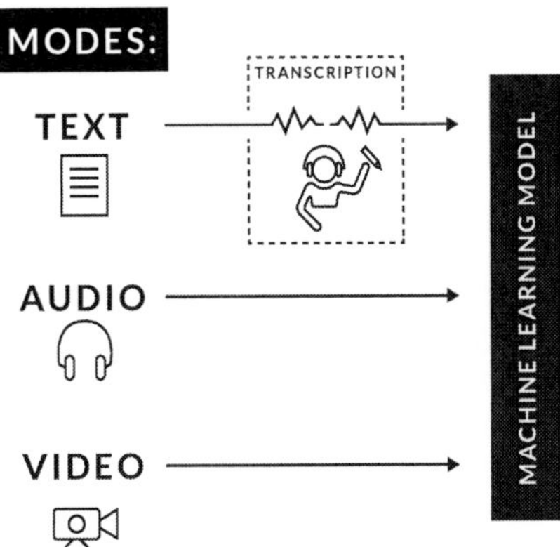

Figure 1: A blindspot in multimodal sentiment analysis is the inclusion of human-transcriptions of spoken sentiment, which limits model applicability. We address this by using only prosodic and visual features for sentiment classification.

1 Introduction

Multimodal fusion models in the spoken-word domain incorporate features outside of text-based natural language processing (NLP) to increase model performance. These models benefit from the full scope of person–person interaction, which provides both context and clarification for speech that is ambiguous as text alone. The addition of multimodal data has been shown to increase model performance across a broad set of spoken-word fields, such as sarcasm (Joshi et al., 2017), question (Donnelly et al., 2017) and sentiment (Zadeh et al., 2017) detection. Each of these examples contains speech that can be difficult to infer from transcribed text—instead, the speaker's intent is clarified to listeners via intonations or expressions. It follows that machine learning models trained to

1

Proceedings of the First Grand Challenge and Workshop on Human Multimodal Language (Challenge-HML), pages 1–10,
Melbourne, Australia July 20, 2018. ©2018 Association for Computational Linguistics

include domain knowledge from these modalities would likewise be able to correctly interpret complex communication.

Multimodal sentiment analysis (MSA) is one example of ambiguous speech that has been shown to benefit from additional modalities (Zadeh et al., 2017, 2018a; Chen et al., 2017; Poria et al., 2017b; Yu et al., 2017). MSA is the identification of the explicit or implicit attitude of a thought or sentence toward a situation or event. In recent years, the online community has been shown to frequently express sentiment orally in videos or recordings uploaded to sites like Youtube or Facebook. These spoken-word opinion pieces have been collected and annotated into large high-quality multimodal sentiment datasets (Zadeh et al., 2016; Busso et al., 2008; Prez-Rosas et al., 2013; Wollmer et al., 2013; Park et al., 2014). Recently, the largest annotated sentiment dataset to date, CMU-MOSEI, was released (Zadeh et al., 2018c). This dataset contains over 23,500 spoken sentence videos, totaling 65 hours, 53 minutes, and 36 seconds. This large quantity of data comes from real-world expressions of sentiment, offering a unique opportunity to train and test model performance and generalization on a large dataset. Additionally, Zadeh et al. (2018b) released a software development kit (SDK) for training and testing models on the CMU-MOSEI dataset, with future work focusing on addition of other multimodal datasets. These releases culminated in a challenge focused on human multimodal language with the opportunity to train a model and evaluate it on a held-out challenge test set.

As is common in sentiment datasets, the MO-SEI dataset includes features from human transcriptions of speech (Soleymani et al., 2017; Poria et al., 2017a). Ideally, models trained to annotate sentiment will operate on real-world data with as few barriers to deployment as possible in order to maximize efficiency and continuity. The use of human transcripts represents one of these barriers—it greatly limits the scalability of models in the real-world due to the time and cost in transcription and the inequality in quality between human and computer transcripts (Morbini et al., 2013; Blanchard et al., 2015).

The goal of this work is to build a model that broadly generalizes to unseen data using only scalable audio and visual features, reducing the need for transcription of human speech. In or-
der to achieve this, we implement a model pipeline which has been successfully deployed in domains of sensitive and affectively impactful video analysis (Moreira et al., 2019). From this pipeline, we select simple high-level video features and a generalized subset of audio features extracted using openSMILE (Eyben et al., 2010). We further test the generalizability of this pipeline by evaluating its applicability to the MSA domain.

Additionally, this pipeline automatically extracts interpretable features that highlight model attention. These features can be easily mapped back to videos, as shown by Moreira et al. (2016), which allows easy interpretation of model performance. Although recent work in MSA has begun exploring applicability of deep learning features, these models mostly achieve high performance numbers in specific scenarios but have poor generalizability and interpretability (Poria et al., 2018).

In the next section, we examine related work on multimodal sentiment analysis. Section 3 explains the model pipeline and evaluation procedure. Section 4 presents our model results on the CMU-MOSEI validation set and the grand challenge held-out test set. Finally, in Section 5 we discuss our results, our model's limitations, and propose future work to improve our model.

2   Related Work

Traditionally, sentiment analysis has been considered a natural language processing (NLP) problem, with data that largely consists of transcribed speech or written essays. The rise of YouTube and other video websites has facilitated an increase in multimodal forms of sentiment expression leading to the release of a number of high-quality video datasets annotated for sentiment (Zadeh et al., 2016; Busso et al., 2008; Prez-Rosas et al., 2013; Wollmer et al., 2013; Park et al., 2014). These datasets have in turn led to an increased interest in multimodal fusion of video, audio, and text modalities for multimodal sentiment analysis (MSA), as summarized in recent surveys (Soleymani et al., 2017; Poria et al., 2017a).

2.1   Sentiment Analysis in the Wild

A known issue with multimodal sentiment analysis (MSA) is the overemphasis on text features as opposed to visual or audio clues (Poria et al., 2017a). In spoken sentiment, text restricts the ap-

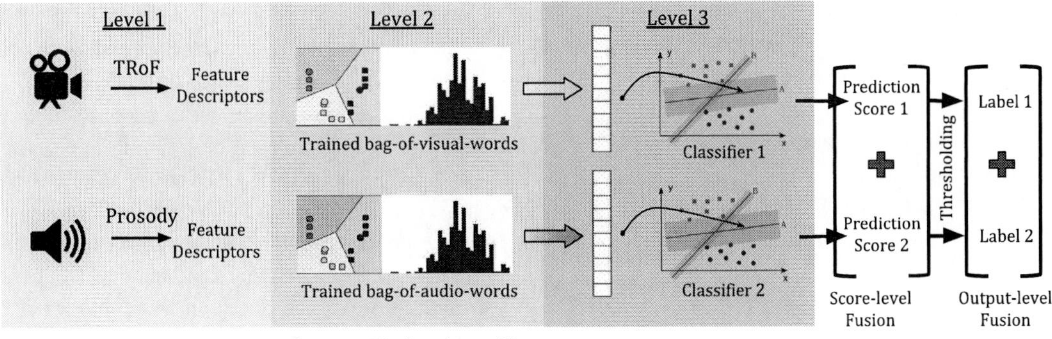

Figure 2: Pipeline of our method with three stages: (i) low-level description of audio/visual stream, (ii) mid-level description of audio/visual stream using a trained bag-of-words model for each modality and (iii) training a classifier to predict class of the features. Fusion can be performed using the second stage features, the third stage score prediction or the thresholded score output labels.

plicability of the model in the wild due to human labor costs of transcription. However, given that a large majority of multimodal sentiment datasets include transcriptions, it is understandable that most researchers in this field have included these features in their models. Rather than minimizing this text-based work, our goal is instead to increase focus on audio and visual modalities as a key area for future MSA research. In this way, we are able to emphasize the real-world scalability of our model by excluding text features. Thus, we limit our review of previous work to recent applications of multimodal fusion of audio and visual features for MSA.

Recent work in MSA using only audio and visual features is relatively sparse, despite the swath of such models in emotion detection (Poria et al., 2017a). Poria et al. (2015) extracted a multitude of frame-level video features and sentence-level audio features for multimodal fusion. They used feature selection to optimize classification of sentiment polarity (positive, negative, or neutral sentiment) and built an audio-visual model that achieved a validation accuracy of 83.69%. Unfortunately, their study contains minimal focus on interpretability of generated and selected features.

Poria et al. (2018) recently published work that established baseline performance on MSA across a range of models and datasets. Their findings confirmed that multimodal audio and visual models have lower performance than multimodal models that contain text. They also found that MSA model performance plummets, regardless

of modality, on cross-dataset tests. Additionally, Poria et al. (2018) presented a machine learning model using audio and video features. They extracted video features using 3D convolution filters, and selected relevant features with a max-pooling operation. Their audio-visual model was evaluated on a variety of datasets, achieving accuracies between 67.90% and 78.80%, depending on the dataset and on training with same-speaker inclusion or not. Additionally, they report their results for various modality fusion techniques, with scores ranging between 58.6% and 65.3%.

The difference between our work and these related works is our method of extracting features from video and representing video segments, which will be detailed in the next section. Additionally, the related works use a large set of audio features provided by openSMILE (Eyben et al., 2010), while we employ only prosodic features for speech analysis, namely fundamental frequency, voicing probability, and loudness contours.

2.2 Model Inspiration and Success in Non-affect Domains

Our approach follows the precedent set by Moreira et al. (2019), who developed a generalized multimodal framework that focuses on robust, handcrafted features. Their architecture provides an efficient and temporally-aware technique for multimodal data processing and has been shown to generalize across different domains, achieving state-of-the-art performance in pornography and violence detection with no human intervention. Inspired by the promising results of this work and interested in further domain applications for the framework, we extract similar features from the MOSEI dataset to build a scalable solution to sentiment analysis in our study.

3 Methods

Sentiment expression and interpretation comprise abstract and complex phenomena, whose translation to audio and visual characteristics is not straightforward. To cope with such complexity in a computationally affordable way (i.e., small runtime and low-memory footprint) we employ a Bag-of-Features-based (BoF) solution to the multimodal sentiment analysis (MSA) domain. BoF models reduce raw data from a modality into a collection of key local features. This technique reduces the semantic gap between the low-level audio and visual data representation, and the high-level concept of sentiment.

Our model training pipeline is presented in Figure 2. Broadly, the pipeline extracts key features from the sentiment sentence videos and computes a confidence score for each modality. Then, the pipeline performs multimodal score fusion, generating a sentiment prediction. Full details can be found in Moreira et al. (2016). Aside from experimenting with different fusion techniques, we performed no hyperparameter tuning in order to test the model's domain adaptation.

One limitation of this training architecture is that currently the feature extraction portion of the framework is only trainable on two class problems. Thus, we binarize sentiment into positive and negative classes. Ideally, this training process will be modified in the future – for now, the ground truth scores are thresholded with values > 0 being positive and ≤ 0 being negative.

The BoF-based feature processing portion of the pipeline is divided into three levels:

Level 1: Low-level Feature Extraction. At this stage we extract low-level features from raw data. In our case, the audio and video streams in the raw videos are first separated and segmented. Temporal Robust Features (TRoF) (Moreira et al., 2016) are then extracted from the video frames. TRoF works by considering Gaussian derivatives for both the spatially and temporally co-located pixels in a set of video frames. Thus, it isolates and captures important spatiotemporal portions for motion description. The pixels of these portions can then be sampled across space and time, prior to being described by regular Speeded-Up Robust Features (SURF) (Bay et al., 2008).

From the audio stream, we extract prosodic features using the sub-harmonic sampling algorithm provided by openSMILE (Eyben et al., 2010). We limit our selection of audio features from openSMILE to correspond with essential features for speech analysis, namely fundamental frequency, voicing probability, and loudness contours of the audio waves. These features have been identified as important in related implementations of the pipeline Moreira et al. (2019).

Level 2: Mid-level Feature Extraction. At this stage we employ a mid-level coding step that quantizes the low-level features according to codebooks. Codebooks are a modular way of representing important features that provide a coarser representation of the video content that is closer and aware of the binarized concept of sentiment. Separate codebooks are created for each modality. For each codebook, we estimate Gaussian Mixture Models (GMM) from one million low-level features, with half of of the features coming from negative-sentiment examples, and the other half coming from positive-sentiment examples. Both GMMs are comprised of 256 Gaussian distributions. After quantization, using the codebook, a pooling step summarizes all of the the mid-level features into a single feature vector for each video segment.

Interpretable features can be extracted from the pipeline using the learned codebook, as described by Moreira et al. (2016).

Level 3: Confidence Generation. Once we obtain the mid-level feature vector for each of our video sentences, a separate linear Support Vector Machine (SVM) classifier is trained for each data modality. In order to optimize the SVM for classification accuracy, we perform a 5-fold cross validation and select the best C, a SVM hyperparameter, using a log_2 scale in the range [-3,15]. Confidence scores are generated using the distance of the samples from the boundary learned by the classifier during training. These scores are then normalized between 0 and 1.

3.1 Prediction Using Multimodal Fusion

Once we obtain confidence scores for each video segment, we employ two late fusion techniques to predict the class of each of the segments. Our methods are inspired by the domain of Biometrics (Ross and Jain, 2003), which has a long history of employing multiple modalities in real-world applications to improve model performance.

1. **Score-level Fusion** The normalized scores for video frame classification and audio signal classification are averaged to obtain our final classification scores. To further extend our fusion-based approach, the weight of each of the two scores contributing to the mean is treated as a hyperparameter, θ. For the validation results we weight both the scores equally and threshold the scores at 0.5 to obtain labels. For evaluation on the test set, we choose the relative weight parameter corresponding to the most accurate validation results. The objective function used to optimize the hyperparameter is defined as:

$$\arg\min_{\theta} \frac{1}{N} \sum_{c=1}^{N} \frac{1}{n_c} \sum_{i=1}^{n_c} I(y_i \neq \hat{y}_i) \quad (1)$$

Here, $\hat{y}_i$ can be defined as:

$$\hat{y}_i = th(\theta * vScore_i + (1-\theta) * aScore_i) \quad (2)$$

Equation 1 denotes the average number of classification errors across all classes. N represents the number of classes (in our case, 2) and n_c corresponds to the number of samples belonging to class c. y_i is the ground truth label and $\hat{y}_i$ is obtained by thresholding the weighted average score as presented in Equation 2. $I(.)$ is an indicator function that takes values 1 when y_i is equal to $\hat{y}_i$. $th(.)$ is the thresholding function that uses $(1-\theta)$ as the threshold corresponding to each value of θ in the equation. The optimized hyperparameter was chosen after testing with grid search in the range [0,1] with a step of 0.2. Here, $\hat{y}_i$ for $\theta = 0$ and $\theta = 1$ correspond to unimodal (either video or audio) classification labels.

2. **Output-level Fusion** This is a simple fusion technique applied through the method of thresholding all of the scores obtained from our classifiers. The thresholded scores are $\in \{-1, 0, 1\}$ and are applied upon uniform binning of the raw confidence scores. We added the thresholded scores for both our modalities and scaled them to a range of 0 to 1. This score was then able to act as the predicted score for a video to belong to a particular class.

3.2 MOSEI

For this work we trained, tested, and validated our model on the MOSEI dataset (Zadeh et al., 2018c). The dataset was composed of over 23,500 spoken sentence videos, totaling 65 hours, 53 minutes, and 36 seconds. The dataset had been segmented at the sentence level; the sentences had been transcribed, and audio, visual, and textual features had been generated and released as part a public Zadeh et al. (2018b) software development kit (SDK). Additionally, raw videos were available for download. Each video had been human scored on two levels: sentiment, which ranges between [-3,3], and emotion, which had six different values. For the purpose of this work, we focused only on the sentiment scores.

For our purposes we extracted features from the raw videos and used the SDK to obtain the dataset's training, testing, and validation sets.

3.3 Evaluation Metrics

Our model output presents predictions as binary positive or negative classes as well as a confidence metric for each video sentence.

We evaluated our model's performance on basic classification of sentiment using precision, recall and F_1-scores. We selected these metrics because they are known to report accurate performance representation on imbalanced classes. Since these metrics are defined for two-classes, we binarize the ground truth scores values by thresholding values > 0 as positive and the remaining as negative.

Although we trained the SVM classifier for binary predictions, the confidence scores obtained from the classifier for each sample are continuous and can be used to perform regression. Since sentiment scores in the dataset scale between [-3, 3], we scaled our confidence scores to match the expected distribution of sentiment using a linear transformation function. These were the predictions that we submitted to the ACL2018 Grand Challenge. We also performed a regression between the ground truth scores and scores obtained by our methods on the validation set, and reported the Mean Absolute Error (MAE) for these experiments alongside our classification results.

Table 1: Performance of individual modality and multimodal fusion for sentiment analysis on the validation set of CMU-MOSEI. MAE is the Mean Absolute Error.

Solution	Precision	Recall	F1-Score	MAE
Audio Prosodic + SVM	0.7485	0.4831	0.5872	0.7919
Video TRoF + SVM	0.7928	0.7198	0.7545	0.7811
Score-level Fusion	**0.8022**	0.5749	0.6698	0.7849
Output-level Fusion	0.7729	**0.8396**	**0.8049**	**0.7760**

4 Results

In this section we present our results on both the MOSEI validation set and the ACL2018 Grand Challenge MOSEI test set. In the validation set section we report the evaluation metrics we used to assess the performance of our model and in the test set section, we present the metrics used by the ACL 2018 Grand Challenge organizers.

4.1 Validation Set Results

Using the metrics of evaluation described in Section. 3.3, we tested our proposed approach on the validation set of the CMU-MOSEI dataset. In general, our model's performance was comparable to related work with the best method achieving F1-score of 0.80. The classification and regression results are presented in Table 1. A finer analysis of correct and wrong classification is presented in Table 3. The video portion of our model performed well on the validation and our fusion techniques resulted in improved performance with respect to using unimodal models. However, the audio-only model performed relatively poorly, indicating that our model's major weakness was in the audio domain. We expand upon this weakness in section 5.1.

4.2 Test Set Results

The classification metrics reported by the organizers on the test set include average F_1-score and average class accuracies considering different numbers of sentiment classes. For regression, they report MAE and the correlation coefficient between ground truth and prediction scores. In the regression scenario, our submission method (Fusion 1) obtained a MAE of 0.91 on the test set and 0.78 on the validation set. The specific metrics and the values achieved by our method on the test set have been reported in Table 2.

Table 2: Performance of the proposed approach in terms of the metric of evaluation used in ACL2018 Human Multimodal Language Challenge

Metric	Value
Mean Average Error (MAE)	0.9108
Correlation Coefficient	0.3051
Average Binary Accuracy	0.6094
Average Weighted Binary Accuracy	0.6108
Average F1 Score	0.6325
Average 5-Class Accuracy	0.3320
Average 7-Class Accuracy	0.3296

We use a binary training technique and correspond the SVM confidence scores to sentiment intensities. However, these results suggest that continuity in our scores does not correspond well with quantized sentiment bins.

5 Limitations and Future Work

In order to be deployed at scale in real-world scenarios, machine learning models should have minimal-to-no human intervention to becoming fully automated. We maximized the automation of our model by discarding human-transcription data, instead relying solely on audio and video features. While this is an important step, we identified three major limitations of our model that should be improved before it is deployed at-scale. First, the quality of our chosen integration of audio features resulted in a poor representation of sentiment. Second, our results show that SVM distance does not map well to sentiment intensity. Third, the CMU-MOSEI dataset pre-segments data into

Table 3: Confusion matrix of classification results from the methods on the validation set of CMU-MOSEI.

↓ Predicted	Actual →	Positive	Negative
	Audio	615	613
Positive	Video	884	344
	Fusion 1	706	522
	Fusion 2	1031	197
	Audio	181	290
Negative	Video	231	240
	Fusion 1	174	297
	Fusion 2	303	168

sentences and omits non-labeled segments. This makes it impossible to obtain a realistic representation of real-world data using only this dataset. By isolating and expanding on these obstacles and their effects on our model's performance, which we do below, we are able to come to noteworthy conclusions that can be incorporated into future work.

5.1 Audio feature limitations

Audio features for our model were selected based on comparison with related work (Moreira et al., 2019). Unfortunately, our multimodal model received relatively little benefit from the audio modality when evaluated on the validation set. We suspect that a major reason for this failure is the relatively poor audio quality of the CMU-MOSEI dataset compared with the dataset used for the related work, which was comprised of production-level videos with Hollywood-level audio qualities.

This is notable as an informative guide to the unforeseen limitations of the previous dataset that related work selected features on (Moreira et al., 2019). Based on that dataset, we limited our model to three audio features. However, Poria et al. (2015) built an audio model which used a large set of audio features (6,373 per video) to obtain a 74.49% classification accuracy for positive, negative, and neutral sentiment. They found that feature selection, which typically improves accuracy, actually decreases audio model performance in the sentiment domain. This suggests that it is better to use as many audio features as possible when building MSA models. We briefly investigated adding more audio features by extract-

ing 384 features from openSmile's emotion feature set (Schuller et al., 2009). Unfortunately, this model only obtained an F1 of 0.51, compared to our model's 0.59. In future work we plan to experiment with audio features further in order to find what works best across domains.

5.2 SVM Distance Limitation

As noted in the results section, the continuous scores generated for predictions using SVM are more granular than the ground truth sentiment scores. When the two are compared, the offset in the scores can lead to higher errors than if they were quantized in the same manner. Based on our observations, we would suggest usage of other techniques for extraction of sentiment intensity.

5.3 Dataset Limitations

The CMU-MOSEI dataset (Zadeh et al., 2018c) used to train and test our model provides a large-scale breakdown of sentiment analysis. However, the dataset follows typical practices for multimodal sentiment datasets, which make it difficult to train a fully automatic model. We identify practices which would increase automation. First, the data is pre-segmented at the sentence level, resulting in no sentenceless data. For a model to be employed in the real-world, it needs to be aware of sentenceless data as well as imperfect sentence boundaries. For example, human often segment speech at the sentence or category level (Stolcke et al., 2000; Zadeh et al., 2016), however, machine learning algorithms have yet to perfect this practice. Previous work has found that NLP models are prone to complete failure when presented with excess words or information, even when those words are unrelated to the task (Jia and Liang, 2017). Ideally, models in the real-world will be robust to such noise.

Second, our model does not use human transcription in order to avoid limitations in real-world applicability. However, text is a modality that improves MSA. Rather than releasing text transcriptions for model building, we propose future datasets release automatic speech recognition transcriptions. This would further model automation by incorporating scalable transcription practices, as is becoming more common in other domains (Blanchard et al., 2016). Additionally, recent work suggests the gap between human transcription and ASR will soon be negated by advances in the speech recognition domain (Stolcke and Droppo,

2017), furthering the argument that human transcription is no longer necessary for building models.

By including the full range of data and switching from human to ASR transcription, we believe that sentiment models can be trained, evaluated, and employed at-scale on real-world data. Work on automating multimodal sentiment analysis should focus on model performance using tractable methods of data collection; as exemplified by other domains intended to work with real-world data (Ram et al., 2018; Yan et al., 2016), with human level transcriptions of data reported as a comparison metric.

6 Conclusion

We conclude our study with the presentation of the results of a generalized model for multimodal sentiment analysis using only visual and audio modalities. In this work, we completed two significant goals: first, we trained and evaluated a MSA model at scale with minimal human intervention. Second, we tested the cross-domain generalizability of a model framework that has shown great success in other multimodal domains. Although multimodal sentiment analysis has traditionally been characterized as a natural language processing field driven by human transcription, we believe that our results show the tractability of models built without human-in-the-loop. We advise researchers to ensure that their future work makes an effort to limit transcript-based datasets by employing automatic speech transcription. By doing this, they will be able to further minimize human interaction and allow their models to approach full automation. This work is one component of a broader effort in the MSA community to expand MSA to process real-world data at scale. Despite the limitations of our model, we believe that our work creates substantial groundwork for further investigation of video- and audio-based models.

References

Herbert Bay, Andreas Ess, Tinne Tuytelaars, and Luc Van Gool. 2008. Speeded-Up Robust Features (SURF). *Computer Vision and Image Understanding* 110(3):346–359. https://doi.org/10.1016/j.cviu.2007.09.014.

Nathaniel Blanchard, Michael Brady, Andrew M. Olney, Marci Glaus, Xiaoyi Sun, Martin Nystrand, Borhan Samei, Sean Kelly, and Sidney D'Mello. 2015. A study of automatic speech recognition in noisy classroom environments for automated dialog analysis. In *International Conference on Artificial Intelligence in Education*. Springer, pages 23–33.

Nathaniel Blanchard, Patrick J. Donnelly, Andrew M. Olney, Borhan Samei, Brooke Ward, Xiaoyi Sun, Sean Kelly, Martin Nystrand, and Sidney K. D'Mello. 2016. Semi-Automatic detection of teacher questions from human-transcripts of audio in live classrooms. In *2016 Ninth International Conference on Educational Data Mining*.

Carlos Busso, Murtaza Bulut, Chi-Chun Lee, Abe Kazemzadeh, Emily Mower, Samuel Kim, Jeannette N. Chang, Sungbok Lee, and Shrikanth S. Narayanan. 2008. IEMOCAP: Interactive emotional dyadic motion capture database. *Language resources and evaluation* 42(4):335.

Minghai Chen, Sen Wang, Paul Pu Liang, Tadas Baltruaitis, Amir Zadeh, and Louis-Philippe Morency. 2017. Multimodal sentiment analysis with word-level fusion and reinforcement learning. In *Proceedings of the 19th ACM International Conference on Multimodal Interaction*. ACM, pages 163–171.

Patrick J. Donnelly, Nathaniel Blanchard, Andrew M. Olney, Sean Kelly, Martin Nystrand, and Sidney K. D'Mello. 2017. Words matter: automatic detection of teacher questions in live classroom discourse using linguistics, acoustics, and context. In *Proceedings of the Seventh International Learning Analytics & Knowledge Conference*. ACM, New York, NY, USA, LAK '17, pages 218–227. https://doi.org/10.1145/3027385.3027417.

Florian Eyben, Martin Wllmer, and Bjrn Schuller. 2010. Opensmile: The Munich Versatile and Fast Open-source Audio Feature Extractor. In *Proceedings of the 18th ACM International Conference on Multimedia*. ACM, New York, NY, USA, MM '10, pages 1459–1462. https://doi.org/10.1145/1873951.1874246.

Robin Jia and Percy Liang. 2017. Adversarial examples for evaluating reading comprehension systems. *arXiv preprint arXiv:1707.07328* .

Aditya Joshi, Pushpak Bhattacharyya, and Mark J. Carman. 2017. Automatic sarcasm detection: A survey. *ACM Computing Surveys (CSUR)* 50(5):73.

Fabrizio Morbini, Kartik Audhkhasi, Kenji Sagae, Ron Artstein, Dogan Can, Panayiotis Georgiou, Shri Narayanan, Anton Leuski, and David Traum. 2013. Which ASR should I choose for my dialogue system? In *Proceedings of the SIGDIAL 2013 Conference*. Metz, France, pages 394–403.

Daniel Moreira, Sandra Avila, Mauricio Perez, Daniel Moraes, Vanessa Testoni, Eduardo Valle, Siome Goldenstein, and Anderson Rocha. 2016. Pornography classification: The hidden clues in video space-time. *Forensic Science International* 268:46–61. https://doi.org/10.1016/j.forsciint.2016.09.010.

Daniel Moreira, Sandra Avila, Mauricio Perez, Daniel Moraes, Vanessa Testoni, Eduardo Valle, Siome Goldenstein, and Anderson Rocha. 2019. Multimodal data fusion for sensitive scene localization. *Information Fusion* 45:307–323. https://doi.org/10.1016/j.inffus.2018.03.001.

Sunghyun Park, Han Suk Shim, Moitreya Chatterjee, Kenji Sagae, and Louis-Philippe Morency. 2014. Computational analysis of persuasiveness in social multimedia: A novel dataset and multimodal prediction approach. In *Proceedings of the 16th International Conference on Multimodal Interaction*. ACM, pages 50–57.

Soujanya Poria, Erik Cambria, Rajiv Bajpai, and Amir Hussain. 2017a. A review of affective computing: From unimodal analysis to multimodal fusion. *Information Fusion* 37:98–125.

Soujanya Poria, Erik Cambria, and Alexander Gelbukh. 2015. Deep convolutional neural network textual features and multiple kernel learning for utterance-level multimodal sentiment analysis. In *Proceedings of the 2015 conference on empirical methods in natural language processing.* pages 2539–2544.

Soujanya Poria, Erik Cambria, Devamanyu Hazarika, Navonil Majumder, Amir Zadeh, and Louis-Philippe Morency. 2017b. Context-dependent sentiment analysis in user-generated videos. In *Proceedings of the 55th Annual Meeting of the Association for Computational Linguistics (Volume 1: Long Papers).* volume 1, pages 873–883.

Soujanya Poria, Navonil Majumder, Devamanyu Hazarika, Erik Cambria, Amir Hussain, and Alexander Gelbukh. 2018. Multimodal Sentiment Analysis: Addressing Key Issues and Setting up Baselines. *arXiv preprint arXiv:1803.07427* .

Vernica Prez-Rosas, Rada Mihalcea, and Louis-Philippe Morency. 2013. Utterance-level multimodal sentiment analysis. In *Proceedings of the 51st Annual Meeting of the Association for Computational Linguistics (Volume 1: Long Papers).* volume 1, pages 973–982.

Ashwin Ram, Rohit Prasad, Chandra Khatri, Anu Venkatesh, Raefer Gabriel, Qing Liu, Jeff Nunn, Behnam Hedayatnia, Ming Cheng, Ashish Nagar, Eric King, Kate Bland, Amanda Wartick, Yi Pan, Han Song, Sk Jayadevan, Gene Hwang, and Art Pettigrue. 2018. Conversational AI: The Science Behind the Alexa Prize. *arXiv:1801.03604 [cs]* ArXiv: 1801.03604. http://arxiv.org/abs/1801.03604.

Arun Ross and Anil Jain. 2003. Information Fusion in Biometrics. *Pattern Recogn. Lett.* 24(13):2115–2125. https://doi.org/10.1016/S0167-8655(03)00079-5.

Björn Schuller, Stefan Steidl, and Anton Batliner. 2009. The interspeech 2009 emotion challenge.

In *Tenth Annual Conference of the International Speech Communication Association.*

Mohammad Soleymani, David Garcia, Brendan Jou, Bjrn Schuller, Shih-Fu Chang, and Maja Pantic. 2017. A survey of multimodal sentiment analysis. *Image and Vision Computing* 65:3 – 14.

Andreas Stolcke, Noah Coccaro, Rebecca Bates, Paul Taylor, Carol Van Ess-Dykema, Klaus Ries, Elizabeth Shriberg, Daniel Jurafsky, Rachel Martin, and Marie Meteer. 2000. Dialogue act modeling for automatic tagging and recognition of conversational speech. *Computational linguistics* 26(3):339–373. http://dl.acm.org/citation.cfm?id=971872.

Andreas Stolcke and Jasha Droppo. 2017. Comparing Human and Machine Errors in Conversational Speech Transcription. *arXiv:1708.08615 [cs]* ArXiv: 1708.08615. http://arxiv.org/abs/1708.08615.

Martin Wollmer, Felix Weninger, Tobias Knaup, Bjorn Schuller, Congkai Sun, Kenji Sagae, and Louis-Philippe Morency. 2013. YouTube Movie Reviews: Sentiment Analysis in an Audio-Visual Context. *IEEE Intelligent Systems* 28(3):46–53. https://doi.org/10.1109/MIS.2013.34.

Jingwei Yan, Wenming Zheng, Zhen Cui, Chuangao Tang, Tong Zhang, Yuan Zong, and Ning Sun. 2016. Multi-clue fusion for emotion recognition in the wild. In *Proceedings of the 18th ACM International Conference on Multimodal Interaction*. ACM, pages 458–463.

Youngjae Yu, Hyungjin Ko, Jongwook Choi, and Gunhee Kim. 2017. End-to-end concept word detection for video captioning, retrieval, and question answering. In *Computer Vision and Pattern Recognition (CVPR), 2017 IEEE Conference on*. IEEE, pages 3261–3269.

Amir Zadeh, Minghai Chen, Soujanya Poria, Erik Cambria, and Louis-Philippe Morency. 2017. Tensor Fusion Network for Multimodal Sentiment Analysis. In *Proceedings of the 2017 Conference on Empirical Methods in Natural Language Processing.* pages 1103–1114.

Amir Zadeh, Paul Pu Liang, Navonil Mazumder, Soujanya Poria, Erik Cambria, and Louis-Philippe Morency. 2018a. Memory Fusion Network for Multi-view Sequential Learning. *arXiv preprint arXiv:1802.00927* .

Amir Zadeh, Paul Pu Liang, Soujanya Poria, Prateek Vij, Erik Cambria, and Louis-Philippe Morency. 2018b. Multi-attention Recurrent Network for Human Communication Comprehension. *arXiv preprint arXiv:1802.00923* .

Amir Zadeh, Paul Pu Liang, Jon Vanbriesen, Soujanya Poria, Erik Cambria, Minghai Chen, and Louis-Philippe Morency. 2018c. Multimodal language analysis in the wild: Cmu-mosei dataset and interpretable dynamic fusion graph. In *Association for Computational Linguistics (ACL)*.

Amir Zadeh, Rowan Zellers, Eli Pincus, and Louis-Philippe Morency. 2016. Multimodal sentiment intensity analysis in videos: Facial gestures and verbal messages. *IEEE Intelligent Systems* 31(6):82–88.

Recognizing Emotions in Video Using Multimodal DNN Feature Fusion

Jennifer Williams, Steven Kleinegesse, Ramona Comanescu, and Oana Radu
Centre for Speech Technology Research (CSTR)
University of Edinburgh, UK
`j.williams@ed.ac.uk`

Abstract

We present our system description of input-level multimodal fusion of audio, video, and text for recognition of emotions and their intensities for the 2018 First Grand Challenge on Computational Modeling of Human Multimodal Language. Our proposed approach is based on input-level feature fusion with sequence learning from Bidirectional Long-Short Term Memory (BLSTM) deep neural networks (DNNs). We show that our fusion approach outperforms unimodal predictors. Our system performs 6-way simultaneous classification and regression, allowing for overlapping emotion labels in a video segment. This leads to an overall binary accuracy of 90%, overall 4-class accuracy of 89.2% and an overall mean-absolute-error (MAE) of 0.12. Our work shows that an early fusion technique can effectively predict the presence of multi-label emotions as well as their coarse-grained intensities. The presented multimodal approach creates a simple and robust baseline on this new Grand Challenge dataset. Furthermore, we provide a detailed analysis of emotion intensity distributions as output from our DNN, as well as a related discussion concerning the inherent difficulty of this task.

1 Introduction

Automatic emotion detection is a longstanding and challenging problem in the field of artificial intelligence and machine learning. One reason why emotion analysis is so difficult is due to the fact that emotions are somewhat subjective, which affects how emotions are perceived and subsequently labeled by human annotators. To compound this even further, the expressed emotions may change, in particular for video data. In addition, multiple emotions can be expressed simultaneously and also as a sequence over time. Emotions provide a type of para-linguistic information that is crucial for many applications in artificial intelligence including: affective speech generation, bio-medical diagnostics, machine translation and human-computer interaction.

Multimodal machine learning has been recently attracting interest, with the abundance of multimedia data available on the internet making it easy for researchers to integrate data of multiple modalities. It is a dynamic research field which aims to integrate and model multiple sources of input, usually acoustic, visual and text.

In order to produce major advances in emotion analysis, there must be adequate techniques for combining and analyzing complex signals. While this notion is applicable across many fields and tasks, in this work we focus on emotion analysis from video data — a very active research area that is beaming with interesting results and methodologies (Pérez-Rosas et al., 2013; Wöllmer et al., 2013; Poria et al., 2015; Brady et al., 2016; Zadeh et al., 2016b). A survey by Baltrušaitis et al. (2018) motivates some of the uses of multimodal analysis, together with five main components:

- **Representation:** Representing and summarizing multimodal data

- **Translation:** Mapping data from one modality to another

- **Alignment:** Identifying relationships between modalities: for example, transcribed text of a video

- **Fusion:** Joining information for different modalities in order to perform a prediction

- **Co-learning:** Exchanging knowledge between modalities

Proceedings of the First Grand Challenge and Workshop on Human Multimodal Language (Challenge-HML), pages 11–19,
Melbourne, Australia July 20, 2018. ©2018 Association for Computational Linguistics

Our work touches on representation, alignment, and co-learning issues, but it is mostly focused on fusion. Specifically, we are interested in finding a way to predict emotions from video data by fusing together three modalities: verbal content, acoustic features and sequences of images. In this work we provide the experimental framework for developing a system for 6-class (multi-label) emotion classification and regression for the First Workshop and Grand Challenge on Computational Modeling of Human Multimodal Language at Association for Computational Linguistics (ACL) 2018. [1]

This paper is organized as follows: in Section 2, we present some relevant work on multimodal emotion recognition. In Section 3 we provide an overview of the CMU-MOSEI dataset and a description of our task. In Section 4, we present our methodology and multimodal fusion technique. In Section 5, we show our experiments and results. In Section 6 we show some analysis of our experiments and in Section 7 we finally discuss and make suggestions for future work.

2   Related Work

In light of recent successes with deep learning approaches to multimodal classification problems (Zadeh et al., 2017), emotion analysis remains truly challenging. Both emotion and sentiment analysis have become increasingly important in recent years. However, it remains a difficult task due to the ambiguity of language and the use of slang and sarcasm (Baltrušaitis et al., 2018; Poria et al., 2017; Soleymani et al., 2017). A persistent idea is that information from other modalities helps to resolve ambiguities, such as adding information about facial features. From the first time that convolutional neural networks (CNNs) were employed for face recognition (Lawrence et al., 1997) to the present times when sentiment analysis revolves around using CNNs (Tripathi et al., 2017; Xu et al., 2014; Pereira et al., November 2016), CNNs appear promising for multimodal sentiment analysis and emotion recognition.

One way to encourage innovation in the area of multimodal emotion analysis is through annual shared tasks. One such task is the Audio Video Emotion Challenge (AVEC) which encourages creative and robust approaches to multi-signal emotion recognition. In 2016, the top-performing emotion recognition system utilized sparse coding as well as a state space estimation approach to multimodal fusion (Brady et al., 2016). Similar to our approach, they used both convolutional networks (CNNs) and recurrent neural networks (RNNs). Their system competed internationally and achieved the top scores for valence and arousal. However, their work was slightly different from ours in that they were working with a different set of signal modalities (audio, video and electro-cardiogram (EEG)) and predicting emotion continuously over time. In addition, the AVEC 2016 Challenge relied on a very small pool of subjects. Our work is based on more than 80 different speakers and our prediction task for videos is conducted on a per-segment basis.

Previous work has shown that there are particular elements of the speech signal which are most indicative of emotional state of the speaker (Chang et al., 2011; Zeng et al., 2009). The features of speech which are most predictive of speaker affect are called low-level descriptors. These low-level descriptors can be extracted from the audio signal using a standard speech toolbox such as the CO-VAREP software (Degottex et al., 2014).

Speech data is often considered sequentially informative. For example, the rise and fall of prosody can form meaningful patterns. Many approaches to detecting emotion in speech use recurrent neural network (RNN) approaches to sequential learning, such as Long-Short Term Memory (LSTM) (Lim et al., 2016). There has been work on emotion recognition using Bidirectional LSTMs, which we also use for developing our best system (e.g. Ghosh et al., 2016; Lee and Tashev, 2015; Han et al., 2014; Chernykh et al., 2017).

There is also considerable work in the area of multi-label emotion recognition for music where the multi-label task has been transformed into sets of one-vs-all (Trohidis et al., 2008). While that approach can be very useful for similar multi-label tasks, we show that our algorithmic approach using DNNs overcomes the need to transform the problem into one-vs-all. Furthermore, we note that there are many ways to evaluate multi-label recognition tasks; in this work however, we followed the metrics set forth by the organizers.

One dataset in particular, called IEMOCAP, is commonly employed for emotion recognition research. It was developed by eliciting specific emotions from subjects while they were being monitored. For example, their facial expressions and

---

[1] http://multicomp.cs.cmu.edu/acl2018multimodalchallenge/

hand movements were recorded while they spoke. The subjects functioned as emotional actors and were asked to perform scripts that were designed to elicit specific emotions: happy, angry, sad, frustrated and neutral (Busso et al., 2008). However, our work uses a slightly broader set of emotions and multiple emotion labels can be activated simultaneously. More importantly, our data is from speakers who have exhibited emotions spontaneously and, according to their own inclination, similar to real-world contexts.

3 Data and Task

In this section we describe the data that we used for developing our Grand Challenge emotion recognition system and more details related to our prediction task.

3.1 Data Description

In an effort to overcome the challenge of consistent emotion labeling, and to allow for meaningful comparison across systems, our work is based on a standardized emotion dataset, called CMU-MOSEI (Zadeh et al., 2018), from the CMU-MultimodalDataSDK toolbox.[2] This dataset contains video segments that were collected 'in the wild' from YouTube wherein the speaker is providing their review of a movie that they have seen. The segments have been labeled by humans for 6 different emotions, including the null case. These labels are: $Anger$, $Disgust$, $Fear$, $Happy$, Sad, and $Surprise$. Each segment can have any combination of emotion labels, or no labels at all. In addition, for each emotion label there is a corresponding regression value in the range of $[0, 3]$ in 9 steps, making step sizes of approximately 0.33 or 1/3. This means that every video segment can be characterized with an emotion as well as the intensity of that emotion.

The CMU-MOSEI dataset (Zadeh et al., 2018) provides pre-processed features and a way to align features; we aligned the data to text throughout all experiments. We chose this because the code for this alignment method was already provided by the CMU-MultimodalSDK toolbox.

Text features consist of word vectors obtained from the Global Vectors for Word Representation (GloVe) software (Pennington et al., 2014) as well as one-hot word representations.

[2]https://github.com/A2Zadeh/CMU-MultimodalDataSDK

Audio features were extracted using the software COVAREP: 12 Mel-frequency cepstral coefficients, pitch tracking and voiced/unvoiced segmenting features, glottal source parameters, peak slope parameters and maxima dispersion quotients. The sampling rate of these features is 100 Hz from the original audio (Degottex et al., 2014)

Video features were extracted using the Emotient FACET software (Littlewort et al., 2011). According to Zadeh et al. (2016a), the visual features include 16 Facial Action Units, 68 Facial Landmarks, Head Pose and Orientation, 6 Basic Emotions and Eye Gaze (Wood et al., 2015; Baltrusaitis et al., 2014). FACET provides frame-by-frame tracking of facial action units. These features are sampled at 30 Hz.

The most common target emotion in our training data is the singleton $Happy$, followed by the $null$ class and the Sad class. The emotion labels can be combined in various ways. For example, the tuples: $(Happy, Sad)$ and $(Anger, Happy)$ both occur with relatively high frequency and are more frequent than the singleton $Fear$.

3.2 Task Description

Using the CMU-MOSEI dataset, we identified our best-performing early fusion prediction system for the emotion recognition Grand Challenge. While the challenge dataset contains emotion labels as well as sentiment labels, our present work is focused entirely on emotion recognition.

Overall our task was to simultaneously predict **emotion label** (none, one, or many) as well as the corresponding **emotion intensity** for each video segment using a fusion of modalities. The exemplar targets can be visualized as follows:

$$target = [0., 0., 0.33, 0.66, 0., 0.]$$

where the array indexes correspond to the set of 6 emotion labels and the continuous values (in steps of 0.33) correspond to intensity. In the above example there are two emotions present simultaneously for this video segment $(Happy, Sad)$, and the two emotions differ in their intensity.

First, we created our own custom data split from the CMU-MOSEI challenge data so that we could utilize a held-out test set. This custom split allowed us to train, validate, and test various ablation groups, compare our models, and identify the best-performing system to use for the emotion recognition Grand Challenge. Otherwise our submission for the Grand Challenge would have relied solely on the performance of a validation set, which may have led to unintentional overfitting when comparing several models.

With our custom split, we had the following distribution of examples: Training: 9400, Validation: 1800, and Testing: 1100, for an approximate split of 76/14/10. To this end, we used our custom data split to experiment with unimodal systems, bimodal systems, and trimodal systems, before submitting our final best-performing model to the Grand Challenge. We used overall mean-absolute error (MAE) as a metric for determining the best model. Finally, our actual system submission to the emotion recognition Grand Challenge was trained, validated, and tested on the standardized data split as provided by the organizers.

4 Methodology

In this section we outline our methodology. First, we describe each of the DNNs that we considered, followed by an explanation of how our system design for input-level multimodal fusion (i.e. early fusion) works. Finally, we provide details regarding feature alignment and DNN hyper-parameters.

4.1 DNN Architectures

CNN: Convolutional Neural Networks are often used in NLP for various prediction tasks, including sentiment analysis (Kim, 2014). The interpretation is not as straightforward as for images, but we can still argue that semantically related vectors will be close to each other within a context window. As outlined later in the methodology, we use one-dimensional Convolutional layers.

LSTM: Recurrent Neural Networks (RNNs) and variants have been proven very successful for many tasks including sentiment analysis on text and are known for their ability to model invariances across time. Recent advancements propose variants of RNNs that do not suffer from the problem of vanishing gradients: Long Short Term Memory (LSTM). The goal of LSTMs is to capture long distance dependencies in a sequence, such as the context words.

Bidirectional LSTM: Bidirectional LSTMs (BLSTMs) increase the amount of available contextual information. The principle is to use both a forward pass and a backward pass through, for instance, a video segment, while treating the features as meaningfully sequential.

4.2 Early Fusion

In the early fusion approach, features from each of the 3 modalities are concatenated at the input-level and together they become the input vector to a DNN — this approach is shown in Figure 1. Since sequences have different lengths, all modalities are processed with a maximum cutoff, in order for the concatenation to be possible. We chose the optimal value for the maximum cutoff by exploring a range of values during the hyper-parameter search. The concatenated features are then fed into a DNN.

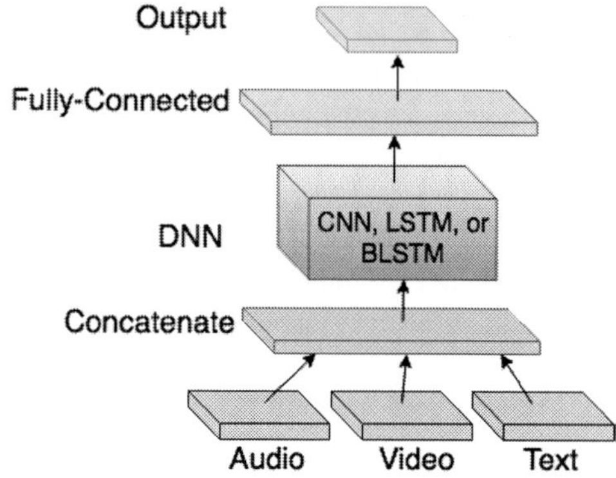

Figure 1: Input-level feature fusion architecture.

4.3 Feature alignment

For our bimodal and trimodal experiments, we align the modalities, because different features in multimodal datasets are in different temporal frequencies. The CMU-MultimodalSDK toolbox aligns data using weighted averaging. The overlap of each modality with a reference one is the weight of each modality. An average is taken with these weights to align them to the reference.

4.4 DNN Hyper-parameters

All of our experiments were trained using the Keras Library (Chollet et al., 2015) which is based on Tensorflow (Abadi et al., 2016). Across all of our experiments, we used the ReLU (Nair and Hinton, 2010) activation function to introduce non-linearity. The learning rule was Adam (Kingma and Ba, 2014) with default Tensorflow parameters. For 1D convolution layers the kernel size was 3 and for max pooling layers the window size was 2. We explored the number of layers in steps of 1, 2 and 3, for both fully connected layers and convolutional layers. For LSTMs and

Bi-directional LSTMs we set the number of units to 64 and for all fully connected layers we set the number of units to 100.

We added dropout (Srivastava et al., 2014) between fully connected layers with dropout rate in $\{0.1, 0.2\}$. We varied the maximum length setting for the video segments in our dataset, known as $maxlen$, in $\{15, 20, 25, 30\}$. We chose these values for maximum length cutoff based on the average segment length reported in Zadeh et al. (2016b), which was indicated as $maxlen = 12$.

In all experiments we used early stopping with the stopping criteria set to identify minimum validation loss and patience was set to 10. The experiments employed batch normalization with batch sizes set to 64 (Ioffe and Szegedy, 2015). The final output layer contained 6 neurons, followed by a linear activation function that bounded values between 0 and 3.

The loss was measured via the mean-absolute error (MAE), where smaller values are better and zero is considered perfect. Our interpretation of MAE is that a value below 0.166 or 1/6 is considerably good performance, based on the intensity range of $[0, 3]$ and the step size of 0.33. Later, we shall describe additional evaluation metrics that were used with our Grand Challenge submission.

5 Experiments

In this section we present the results of our experiments on a random prediction baseline, followed by unimodal, bimodal and trimodal input-level feature fusion. We used the outcome of these experiments to evaluate and compare each model perfomance. Finally, we provide the results for the Grand Challenge from our best-performing system: the trimodal BLSTM.

5.1 Random Baseline

Developing a baseline was motivated by the fact that this is the first shared-task on the CMU-MOSEI dataset, and therefore no existing systems are available for a direct comparison. There are several different ways of developing a baseline on this task: (1) fully-randomized, (2) preserving label-category distributions from training data or (3) preserving label-quantity distributions from training data. We developed a fully-randomized baseline because it is the most trivial model. Our random baseline methodology can be easily adapted to other metrics used by the shared-

Emotion	MAE
Anger	0.70
Disgust	0.68
Fear	0.62
Happy	0.80
Sad	0.72
Surprise	0.05
Overall	**0.60**

Table 1: Baseline MAE based on randomized predictions of quantity of labels, label category, and intensity.

task organizers, such as 4-class accuracy.

First, we generated a random number n for the quantity of labels present in a given video segment from the domain $n = \{0, 1, 2, 3, 4, 5, 6\}$ so that none or all emotion labels could potentially be predicted. Given this quantity, we predicted the identity of the labels by randomly choosing n labels from the domain $[Anger, Disgust, Fear, Happy, Sad, Surprised]$. Finally, we randomly predicted an intensity for each label based on the 9-step regression values in the range of $[0, 3]$, with step size 0.33. The result was an array for each video segment which we used to compare with the truth labels in our small, held-out test set. Table 1 displays our per-label prediction values in terms of MAE. Therefore we can say that if a system performs better than overall MAE of 0.60 (lower values are better) then it is performing better than pure chance.

5.2 Unimodal

To begin with, we experimented with unimodal approaches to set another performance baseline and to find out if any particular modality seemed to contribute significantly more, or if performance was skewed. The results for unimodal performances of each DNN can be found in Table 2. We used our custom training/validation/test split of the available data to obtain this performance, where the overall MAE is only reported on a small held-out test set (but not the official Grand Challenge test set). The performance metric MAE has been averaged over all of the 6 emotion label classes.

The audio modality performed best with a CNN. On the other hand, both text and video performed better with LSTMs. This suggests that text and video provide learnable structures that are captured with sequence modeling.

Modality	DNN	Overall MAE
Audio	LSTM	0.150
	BLSTM	0.150
	CNN	**0.146**
Video	**LSTM**	**0.146**
	BLSTM	0.147
	CNN	0.149
Text	**LSTM**	**0.156**
	BLSTM	0.157
	CNN	0.158

Table 2: Unimodal prediction results, overall mean-absolute error (MAE) for each DNN.

Modality	DNN	Overall MAE
Audio+Video	LSTM	0.137
	BLSTM	**0.135**
	CNN	0.138
Audio+Text	**LSTM**	**0.140**
	BLSTM	0.142
	CNN	0.146
Text+Video	LSTM	0.149
	BLSTM	**0.145**
	CNN	0.149

Table 3: Bimodal prediction results, overall mean-absolute error (MAE) for each DNN and ablation.

5.3 Bimodal

For each bimodal ablation group model, we combined two of the three modalities with a DNN. We report the results in Table 3. We used our custom train/valid/test split of the available data to obtain this performance. We observe that overall, the bimodal ablations performed slightly better than single modalities in terms of overall MAE. The audio+video ablation group performed better than other modality pairs. This could be related to the ambiguity of spoken language. Emotions that embody sarcasm, irony, and typical spoken disfluencies may be better captured without the noise of the text. Text can be particularly misleading in cases of sarcasm, where the truth-value of a sentence is reverse from its literal interpretation.

5.4 Trimodal

We present the results of our trimodal fusion in Table 4. Once again, we used our custom training/validation/test split of the available data to obtain this performance. It is interesting to note that all of these systems performed similarly well,

and all performed better than the bimodal ablation groups. Based on the results from our trimodal experiments, we selected the BLSTM to submit as our system to the Grand Challenge.

DNN	Modality	Overall MAE
LSTM	A,V,T	0.133
BLSTM	**A,V,T**	**0.132**
CNN	A,V,T	0.134

Table 4: Trimodal prediction results, overall MAE for each DNN. Note A=Audio, V=Video, and T=Text.

5.5 Grand Challenge Results

To obtain the official Grand Challenge results, we trained our BLSTM using the original dataset split as provided by the organizers for training and validation. We then applied our system model to an unseen test set and submitted our predictions. The evaluation results were returned to us by the challenge organizers.

Our system performance is displayed in Table 5. It shows the performance on a per-emotion basis as well as the overall metric. We noticed that our system's overall performance, in terms of MAE, on this held-out test set was slightly better than what we obtained while constructing our model during earlier experiments. This could be due to the fact that we used the entire provided training and validation set for the submission.

First, binary accuracy was calculated by rounding values to the nearest integer, and using non-zeros for the 'positive' class and zeros as the 'negative' class. Binary accuracy is used to measure the presence and absence of an emotion label. Next, the 4-class accuracy is obtained in a similar way. Each value is rounded to the nearest integer in $\{0, 1, 2, 3\}$ resulting in 4 classes. And the accuracy is again measured on exact matches. The 4-class accuracy provides a rough estimate of how well a system predicts intensity of an emotion because the 4-classes provide a coarser-step size within the range of regression values (e.g. 4 steps in the range [0,3] instead of 9 steps). Finally, the correlation r is provided for a fine-grained metric that measures how well the system output correlates with the true intensities from the data.

For each emotion label, our correlation values are near 0, which indicates that our system outputs do not correlate with fine-grained emotion inten-

Emotion	MAE	Binary Acc(%)	4-class Acc(%)	Corr. r
Anger	0.101	92.6	92.6	0.082
Disgust	0.051	96.3	96.3	0.064
Fear	0.051	95.7	95.7	0.011
Happy	0.404	70.5	62.0	0.551
Sad	0.111	91.0	91.0	-0.062
Surprise	0.038	97.7	97.7	-0.030
Overall	**0.126**	**90.6**	**89.2**	–

Table 5: Official Grand Challenge system results for our early-fusion trimodal BLSTM.

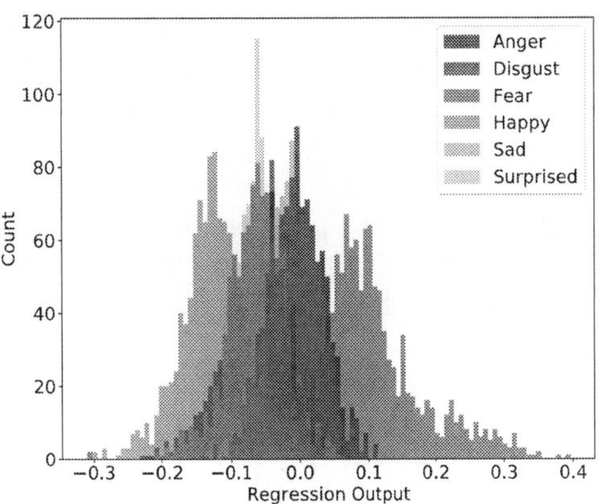

Figure 2: Distribution of predicted intensity targets for each emotion: $[Anger, Disgust, Fear, Happy, Sad, Surprised]$

sity values from the dataset. However, in the presence of relatively high 4-class accuracy, we know that our system is correctly predicting which emotions are present most of the time, and can produce the correct intensity at a coarser-grained step size.

6 Analysis

Unfortunately we were not able to obtain information about the distribution of emotion classes contained in the held-out test set. However, we did observe interesting combinations of emotion label clusters from our training data. More than 70% of the training examples had been labeled with only 1 or 2 emotions, for example: $(Happy, Surprise)$, $(Anger, Disgust)$, $(Disgust, Sad)$ or $(Fear, Sad)$. At the same time, the null case (no emotion) was the second-most prevalent label meaning that many of the video segments in our training data had no emotion at all. There were a few rare cases of interesting combinations, such as all 6 emotions being present in one video segment. This exemplifies the inherent complexity and challenge of human communication and the task of emotion labeling.

In Figure 2, we show the distribution of log-predicted emotion intensities for each of the 6 emotion classes. The BLSTM model appears to have learned a representation where the tuple emotions of $(Surprise, Disgust)$ and $(Anger, Fear)$ each have a similar intensity distribution. Intuitively, this could be justified because these pairs are close to each other on the emotional spectrum, e.g. $Surprise$ is easily mistaken for $Disgust$. Our model however, performs best when distinguishing between $Surprise$ and $Disgust$, implying that although the one-dimensional intensity appears similar in Figure 2, the underlying representation that is learned is complex enough to dis-

tinguish between these. At the same time, Figure 2 implies that the model has learned that $Fear$ and $Happy$ are extremely different emotions, seeing as their corresponding distributions are far apart, which is also intuitive.

7 Discussion and Future Work

We have presented our efforts towards creating a robust and effective emotion recognition system. Our best system predicts emotion in video by performing both classification and regression on this challenging multi-label problem. As this is the first grand challenge for this dataset, we were not able to make a direct comparison between other systems at this time. However, our methodology shows that our models improve simply by adding additional modalities. Furthermore, all of our DNN models perform better than chance. To that end, we know that trimodal models perform best, followed by bimodal models and then unimodal models. Our work shows that an early fusion technique can effectively predict the presence of multi-label emotions as well as their coarse-grained intensities. Our approach creates a simple and robust baseline on this new dataset.

In future work, we propose exploring feature selection in order to better understand if and how particular modality features correlate with particular emotions. For example, in the audio modality, a falling pitch might indicate Sad, or a loud volume could indicate $Surprise$. Capturing features that correlate with particular emotions could prove useful for generating emotive speech.

We have shown that this problem benefits from sequence information. Therefore, in future efforts to improve performance, one might explore the distribution of emotions across video segments. It is possible that there are relevant patterns of emotion that are expressed from one segment to the next. A potential approach for this would be to use a fixed-width sliding window across multiple consecutive video segments, and predict emotion labels at regular time intervals.

Acknowledgments

This work was supported in part by the EPSRC Centre for Doctoral Training in Data Science, funded by the UK Engineering and Physical Sciences Research Council (grant EP/L016427/1) and the University of Edinburgh. The authors would like to thank Steve Renals at University of Edinburgh Centre for Speech Technology Research (CSTR) and the anonymous reviewers for their valuable comments.

References

Martín Abadi, Paul Barham, Jianmin Chen, Zhifeng Chen, Andy Davis, Jeffrey Dean, Matthieu Devin, Sanjay Ghemawat, Geoffrey Irving, Michael Isard, et al. 2016. Tensorflow: A System For Large-Scale Machine Learning. In *Proceedings of the 12th USENIX conference on Operating Systems Design and Implementation*, pages 265–283. USENIX Association.

Tadas Baltrušaitis, Chaitanya Ahuja, and Louis-Philippe Morency. 2018. Multimodal Machine Learning: A Survey and Taxonomy. *IEEE Transactions on Pattern Analysis and Machine Intelligence*.

Tadas Baltrusaitis, Peter Robinson, and Louis-Philippe Morency. 2014. Continuous Conditional Neural Fields for Structured Regression. In *Computer Vision - ECCV 2014 - 13th European Conference, Zurich, Switzerland, September 6-12, 2014, Proceedings, Part IV*, pages 593–608.

Kevin Brady, Youngjune Gwon, Pooya Khorrami, Elizabeth Godoy, William Campbell, Charlie Dagli, and Thomas S Huang. 2016. Multi-Modal Audio, Video and Physiological Sensor Learning for Continuous Emotion Prediction. In *Proceedings of the 6th International Workshop on Audio/Visual Emotion Challenge (AVEC)*, pages 97–104. ACM.

Carlos Busso, Murtaza Bulut, Chi-Chun Lee, Abe Kazemzadeh, Emily Mower, Samuel Kim, Jeannette N Chang, Sungbok Lee, and Shrikanth S Narayanan. 2008. IEMOCAP: Interactive Emotional Dyadic Motion Capture Database. *Language Resources and Evaluation (LREC)*, 42(4):335.

Keng-hao Chang, Drew Fisher, and John Canny. 2011. AMMON: A Speech Analysis Library For Analyzing Affect, Stress, and Mental Health on Mobile Phones. *Proceedings of PhoneSense*.

Vladimir Chernykh, Grigoriy Sterling, and Pavel Prihodko. 2017. Emotion Recognition from Speech With Recurrent Neural Networks. *arXiv preprint arXiv:1701.08071*.

François Chollet et al. 2015. Keras. https://keras.io.

Gilles Degottex, John Kane, Thomas Drugman, Tuomo Raitio, and Stefan Scherer. 2014. COVAREP a Collaborative Voice Analysis Repository for Speech Technologies. In *IEEE International Conference on Acoustics, Speech and Signal Processing (ICASSP), 2014*, pages 960–964. IEEE.

Sayan Ghosh, Eugene Laksana, Louis-Philippe Morency, and Stefan Scherer. 2016. Representation learning for speech emotion recognition. In *INTERSPEECH*, pages 3603–3607.

Kun Han, Dong Yu, and Ivan Tashev. 2014. Speech Emotion Recognition Using Deep Neural Network and Extreme Learning Machine. In *INTERSPEECH 2014, Fifteenth Annual Conference of the International Speech Communication Association (ISCA)*.

Sergey Ioffe and Christian Szegedy. 2015. Batch Normalization: Accelerating Deep Network Training by Reducing Internal Covariate Shift. In *International Conference on Machine Learning*, pages 448–456.

Yoon Kim. 2014. Convolutional Neural Networks for Sentence Classification. *CoRR*, abs/1408.5882.

Diederik Kingma and Jimmy Ba. 2014. Adam: A Method for Stochastic Optimization. *arXiv preprint arXiv:1412.6980*.

Steve Lawrence, C. Lee Giles, Ah Chung Tsoi, and Andrew D. Back. 1997. Face Recognition: A Convolutional Neural-Network Approach. *IEEE Transactions on Neural Networks*, 8(1):98–113.

Jinkyu Lee and Ivan Tashev. 2015. High-Level Feature Representation Using Recurrent Neural Network for Speech Emotion Recognition. In *INTERSPEECH 2015, Sixteenth Annual Conference of the International Speech Communication Association (ISCA)*.

Wootaek Lim, Daeyoung Jang, and Taejin Lee. 2016. Speech Emotion Recognition Using Convolutional and Recurrent Neural Networks. In *Signal and Information Processing Association Annual Summit and Conference (APSIPA), 2016 Asia-Pacific*, pages 1–4. IEEE.

Gwen Littlewort, Jacob Whitehill, Tingfan Wu, Ian R. Fasel, Mark G. Frank, Javier R. Movellan, and Marian Stewart Bartlett. 2011. The Computer Expression Recognition Toolbox (CERT). In *Ninth IEEE International Conference on Automatic Face and*

Gesture Recognition (FG 2011), Santa Barbara, CA, USA, 21-25 March 2011, pages 298–305.

Vinod Nair and Geoffrey E. Hinton. 2010. Rectified Linear Units Improve Restricted Boltzmann Machines. In *Proceedings of the 27th International Conference on International Conference on Machine Learning*, ICML'10, pages 807–814, USA.

Jeffrey Pennington, Richard Socher, and Christopher D. Manning. 2014. GloVe: Global Vectors for Word Representation. In *Empirical Methods in Natural Language Processing (EMNLP)*, pages 1532–1543.

Moisés H. R. Pereira, Flávio L.C. Pádua, Adriano C.M. Pereira, Fabrício Benevenuto, and Daniel H. Dalip. November 2016. Fusing Audio, Textual and Visual Features for Sentiment Analysis of News Videos. *Tenth International AAAI Conference on Web and Social Media (ICWSM)*, pages pp. 17–20.

Verónica Pérez-Rosas, Rada Mihalcea, and Louis-Philippe Morency. 2013. Utterance-Level Multimodal Sentiment Analysis. In *Proceedings of the 51st Annual Meeting of the Association for Computational Linguistics (Volume 1: Long Papers)*, volume 1, pages 973–982.

Soujanya Poria, Erik Cambria, Rajiv Bajpai, and Amir Hussain. 2017. A Review of Affective Computing: From Unimodal Analysis to Multimodal Fusion. *Information Fusion*, 37:98–125.

Soujanya Poria, Erik Cambria, and Alexander Gelbukh. 2015. Deep Convolutional Neural Network Textual Features and Multiple Kernel Learning for Utterance-Level Multimodal Sentiment Analysis. In *Proceedings Empirical Methods in Natural Language Processing (EMNLP)*, pages 2539–2544.

Mohammad Soleymani, David Garcia, Brendan Jou, Björn Schuller, Shih-Fu Chang, and Maja Pantic. 2017. A Survey of Multimodal Sentiment Analysis. *Image and Vision Computing*, 65:3–14.

Nitish Srivastava, Geoffrey Hinton, Alex Krizhevsky, Ilya Sutskever, and Ruslan Salakhutdinov. 2014. Dropout: A simple way to prevent neural networks from overfitting. *Journal of Machine Learning Research*, 15:1929–1958.

Samarth Tripathi, Shrinivas Acharya, Ranti Dev Sharma, Sudhanshu Mittal, and Samit Bhattacharya. 2017. Using Deep and Convolutional Neural Networks for Accurate emotion classification on DEAP Dataset. In *Proceedings of the Thirty-First AAAI Conference on Artificial Intelligence, February 4-9, 2017, San Francisco, California, USA.*, pages 4746–4752.

Konstantinos Trohidis, Grigorios Tsoumakas, George Kalliris, and Ioannis P. Vlahavas. 2008. Multi-Label Classification of Music into Emotions. In *International Society of Music Information Retrieval (IS-MIR)*, volume 8, pages 325–330.

Martin Wöllmer, Felix Weninger, Tobias Knaup, Björn Schuller, Congkai Sun, Kenji Sagae, and Louis-Philippe Morency. 2013. Youtube Movie Reviews: Sentiment Analysis in an Audio-Visual Context. *IEEE Intelligent Systems*, 28(3):46–53.

Erroll Wood, Tadas Baltrusaitis, Xucong Zhang, Yusuke Sugano, Peter Robinson, and Andreas Bulling. 2015. Rendering of Eyes for Eye-Shape Registration and Gaze Estimation. In *Proceedings of the IEEE International Conference on Computer Vision*, pages 3756–3764.

Can Xu, Suleyman Cetintas, Kuang-Chih Lee, and Li-Jia Li. 2014. Visual Sentiment Prediction with Deep Convolutional Neural Networks. *CoRR*, abs/1411.5731.

Amir Zadeh, Minghai Chen, Soujanya Poria, Erik Cambria, and Louis-Philippe Morency. 2017. Tensor fusion network for multimodal sentiment analysis. *CoRR*, abs/1707.07250.

Amir Zadeh, Paul Pu Liang, Jon Vanbriesen, Soujanya Poria, Erik Cambria, Minghai Chen, and Louis-Philippe Morency. 2018. Multimodal language Analysis in the Wild: CMU-MOSEI Dataset and Interpretable Dynamic Fusion Graph. In *Association for Computational Linguistics (ACL)*.

Amir Zadeh, Rowan Zellers, Eli Pincus, and Louis-Philippe Morency. 2016a. MOSI: Multimodal Corpus of Sentiment Intensity and Subjectivity Analysis in Online Opinion Videos. *CoRR*, abs/1606.06259.

Amir Zadeh, Rowan Zellers, Eli Pincus, and Louis-Philippe Morency. 2016b. Multimodal Sentiment Intensity Analysis in Videos: Facial Gestures and Verbal Messages. *IEEE Intelligent Systems*, 31(6):82–88.

Zhihong Zeng, Maja Pantic, Glenn I Roisman, and Thomas S Huang. 2009. A Survey of Affect Recognition Methods: Audio, Visual, and Spontaneous Expressions. *IEEE Transactions on Pattern Analysis and Machine Intelligence*, 31(1):39–58.

Multimodal Relational Tensor Network for Sentiment and Emotion Classification

Saurav Sahay **Shachi H Kumar** **Rui Xia** **Jonathan Huang** **Lama Nachman**
Anticipatory Computing Lab
Intel Labs
{saurav.sahay, shachi.h.kumar, rui.xia, Jonathan.Huang, lama.nachman}
@intel.com

Abstract

Understanding Affect from video segments has brought researchers from the language, audio and video domains together. Most of the current multimodal research in this area deals with various techniques to fuse the modalities, and mostly treat the segments of a video independently. Motivated by the work of (Zadeh et al., 2017) and (Poria et al., 2017), we present Relational Tensor Network architecture where we use the inter-modal interactions within a segment and also consider the sequence of segments in a video to model the inter-segment inter-modal interactions. We also generate rich representations of text and audio modalities by leveraging richer audio and linguistic context alongwith fusing fine-grained knowledge based polarity scores from text. We present the results of our model on CMU-MOSEI dataset and show that our model outperforms many baselines and state of the art methods for sentiment classification and emotion recognition.

1 Introduction

Sentiment Analysis is broadly defined as the computational study of subjective elements such as opinions, attitudes, and emotions towards other objects or persons. Sentiments attach to modalities such as text, audio and video at different levels of granularity and are useful in deriving social insights about various entities such as movies, products, persons or organizations. Emotion Understanding is another closely related field that commonly deals with analysis of audio, video, and other sensory signals for getting psychological and behavioral insights about an individual's mental state. Emotions are defined as brief organically synchronized evaluations of major events

whereas sentiments on the other hand are considered as more enduring beliefs and dispositions towards objects or persons (Scherer, 1984). The field of Emotion Understanding has rich literature with many interesting models of understanding (Plutchik, 2001) (Ekman, 2009) (Posner et al., 2005).

In this work, we explore methods that combine various unimodal techniques for classification alongwith multimodal techniques for fusion of cross modal interactions to perform sentiment analysis and emotion understanding. We develop and test our approaches on the CMU-MOSEI dataset (Zadeh et al., 2018d) as part of the ACL Multimodal Emotion Recognition grand challenge. CMU Multimodal Opinion Sentiment and Emotion Intensity (CMU-MOSEI) dataset is a newly released large dataset of multimodal sentiment analysis and emotion recognition on YouTube video segments. The dataset contains more than 23,500 sentence utterance videos from more than 1000 online YouTube speakers. The dataset has several interesting properties such as being gender balanced, containing various topics and monologue videos from people with different personality traits. The videos are manually transcribed and properly punctuated. Since the dataset comprises of natural audio-visual opinionated expressions of the speakers, it provides an excellent testbed for research in emotion and sentiment understanding. The videos are cut into continuous segments and the segments are annotated with 7 point scale sentiment labels and 4 point scale emotion categories corresponding to the Eckman'a 6 basic emotion classes (EKMAN, 2002). The opinionated expressions in the segments contain visual cues, audio variations in signal as well textual expressions showing various subtle and non-obvious interactions across the modalities for both sentiment and emotion classification.

What differentiates our work from existing lit-

Proceedings of the First Grand Challenge and Workshop on Human Multimodal Language (Challenge-HML), pages 20–27,
Melbourne, Australia July 20, 2018. ©2018 Association for Computational Linguistics

erature is (i) application of a novel cross modal fusion technique across the temporal segments of the multimodal channel (ii) use of rich shallow semantic domain knowledge that include a large number of psycholinguistic features and resources for sentiment and emotion classification and (iii) extraction of emotion aware acoustic phoneme level features using a novel method and architecture.

Our unimodal research focus in this paper is an exploration of speech sentiment and emotion recognition using various text dependent and text independent techniques. On the text modality experiments, we've explored (i) fusion of Lexicons as additional input features (ii) fusion of polarity discriminating lexico-syntactic fine-grained scores as additional input features (iii) fusion of rich contextualized embeddings as additional input features to the classification pipeline. On audio modality, we've used a novel pipeline to generate the iVectors and Phoneme level utterance features. For fusion of multimodal information, we have explored techniques that leverage intra-modal and inter-modal dynamics and fused them together in a novel Relational Tensor Network architecture.

2   Related Work

Sentiment Analysis has received a lot of prior attention in Movie reviews and Product reviews domain and is an established field of research in NLP (Liu, 2010) (Pang and Lee, 2008). However, this hasn't been widely researched in conversational multimodal audio-visual and textual context for continuous recognition of sentiments and emotions. (Kaushik et al., 2013) perform sentiment extraction on natural audio streams using ASR on Youtube videos. They use a maximum entropy classifier and do not use any lexicon features or do any domain adaptation. Multimodal Affect recognition has lately gained a lot of popularity with release of multiple datasets and approaches (Zadeh et al., 2018c) (Zadeh et al., 2018b). (Zadeh et al., 2017) present a tensor fusion technique to generate a fused representation of the individual modalities. Most of these techniques treat the segments of a video independently and ignore the temporal relations and interactions between the segments of a video. (Poria et al., 2017) present an LSTM based network architecture that leverages the context or the temporal interactions between neighboring segments of a video by concatenation of

cross modal features across the segments. For acoustic emotion recognition, one of the most successful system is based on the super-segmental acoustic features which is extracted by applying multiple functions on frame-level features. These features have been adopted as the baseline system in many acoustic emotion challenges (Schuller et al., 2016) (Valstar et al., 2016) (Dhall et al., 2013). Deep learning techniques have also been used in acoustic emotion recognition system in recent years. In (Neumann and Vu, 2017), convolutional neural network (CNN) is applied on the frame-level feature. In (Tao and Liu, 2017), recurrent neural network (RNN) is used to model the temporal information for emotion recognition system.

3   Model Description

This work brings together techniques for various modality specific feature extraction methods and fusion of information from different modalities for Sentiment and Emotion Classification. The grand challenge dataset comes with modality specific features for text, audio and images as a part of the CMU Multimodal Data SDK (Zadeh et al., 2018a). The text features are based on Glove embeddings (Pennington et al., 2014), audio features are based on COVAREP (Degottex et al., 2014)and the visual features based on FACET (Baltruaitis et al., 2016) visual feature extraction libraries. We extracted various additional features for text and audio modalities as described in the following sections.

3.1   Text

Several traditional methods have been developed in Sentiment Analysis technology for decades before the recent advances in deep learning that primarily rely on methods for word vector representation and automated feature discovery from snippets. We look at modeling some of the traditional methods and features in the deep pipeline and study the impact of these on the classifiers. Below, we describe a couple of traditional knowledge based resources alongwith some recent deep representations that we have fused together in our pipeline.

3.1.1   Lexico-syntactic Rule based features

Text is processed to intrinsically understand the deeper lexico-syntactic patterns to relate them

```
I feel very good about this
{'compound': 0.4927, 'neg': 0.0, 'pos': 0.444, 'neu': 0.556}
I feel VERY good about this
{'compound': 0.6028, 'neg': 0.0, 'pos': 0.495, 'neu': 0.505}
I feel very good about this!!!
{'compound': 0.6211, 'neg': 0.0, 'pos': 0.504, 'neu': 0.496}
I feel great about this
{'compound': 0.6249, 'neg': 0.0, 'pos': 0.577, 'neu': 0.423}
I feel GREAT about this!! :)
{'compound': 0.8561, 'neg': 0.0, 'pos': 0.737, 'neu': 0.263}
```

Figure 1: Sentiment Analyzer

with world knowledge to extract meaningful inferences such as sentiments and emotions. We have explored the use of VADER rules (Hutto and Gilbert, 2014) for sentiment and emotion induction. VADER is a simple and fast rule-based model for general sentiment analysis. It utilizes a human-validated general sentiment lexicon and general rules related to grammar and syntax. The goal of this work is to capture generalizable rules and heuristics associated with grammatical and syntactical cues people use to assess sentiment intensity in text. We can clearly see from Figure 1 how this system can differentiate emphasis, intensity and non-linguistic cues from utterances. Deep learning based systems today fail to capture such systematic nuances deterministically.

3.1.2 Sentiment Lexicons

Lexicons consists of maps of key-value pairs, where the key is a word and the value is a list of sentiment scores for that word (e.g., probabilities of the word in positive, neutral, and negative contexts). The scores have different ranges for showing very negative to very positive sentiments. Lexicon embeddings are sparse signals derived by taking the normalized scores from multiple sources of lexicon datasets. The simplest method of blending a lexicon embedding into its corresponding word embedding is to append it to the end of the word embedding. The General Inquirer(GI) (Stone et al., 1966) is a text analysis application with one of the oldest manually constructed lexicons still in widespread use. It contains 11000 words in 183 different psycho-linguistic categories. We have used the lexicon based General Inquirer classes that are divided into groups such as valence, semantic dimensions, cognitive orientation, institutional context, motivation related words, classes of Power, Respect, Affection, Wealth, Well-being, Enlightenment, Skill, etc.. (Shin et al., 2017) who originally explored this work in depth show that lexicon embeddings allow building high-performing

models with much smaller word embeddings.

3.1.3 Contextualized Language Embeddings

In contrast to the above two features, we have also looked at recent developments in contextualized deep word vector representations and how they can help with sentiment and emotion classification. These word vectors are learned functions of the internal states of a deep bidirectional language model, which is pretrained on a large text corpus. The additional language modeling views to vector generation process results in high quality representations (Peters et al., 2018). These word vector representations try to model the complex characteristics of word use along with how these uses vary across linguistic contexts (i.e., to model polysemy). We have used ELMo that learns a linear combination of the vectors stacked above each input word for each end task, which improves performance over just using the top LSTM layer (McCann et al., 2017) . Unlike most widely used word embeddings (Pennington et al., 2014), ELMo word representations are functions of the entire input sentence

3.2 Audio Features

For this task, three different kinds of features were applied. The first one is the feature set extracted by using COVAREP which is provided by the challenge. It includes multiple kinds of frame level acoustic features, such as Mel-frequency Cepstral Coefficients (MFCCs), energy and etc. More details are described in (Gusfield, 1997). Along with COVAREP features, we proposed two additional feature-sets, i-vector features and phoneme level features. Following two sections will discuss details about proposed feature-sets.

3.2.1 I-vector Features

The previous studies (Xia and Liu, 2016) (Tao et al., 2018) have shown that i-vector feature can benefit acoustic emotion recognition system. I-vector modeling is a technique to map the high dimensional Gaussian Mixture Model (GMM) supervector space (generated by concatenating the mean of the mixtures from GMM) to low dimensional space called total variability space T.

Give an utterance u, x_t^u which represents t-th frame of utterance u. Audio frame x_t^u is generated by the following distribution:

$$x_t^u \sim \sum_c p(c|x_t^u)\mathcal{N}(m_c + Tw^u, \Sigma_c) \quad (1)$$

where $p(c|x_t^u)$ is the posterior probability of c-th Gaussian in Universal Background Model (UBM), m_c and Σ_c represent the means and covariance of c-th Gaussian and w^u is the latent i-vector for utterance u. EM algorithm introduced in is applied to iteratively train T. Note that UBM is a GMM which trained with a large corpus.

In (Lei et al., 2014), the phonetically-aware DNN is used to replace the traditional UBM in the framework of i-vector training which showed significant improvements on the speaker identification task. The phonetically-aware DNN is the network for the acoustic model of the Automatic Speech Recognition (ASR) system. It is trained for recognizing the tri-phone state. Compared to the traditional trained UBM, the DNN from ASR represents the feature space constrained on pre-defined tri-phone states. The posterior probability as the output of this DNN is directly used as the $p(c|x_t^u)$ in Equation 1. In this work, ASR and i-vector extractor are pre-trained on Librispeech dataset (Panayotov et al., 2015) with Kaldi (Povey et al., 2011). We used 960 hours speech data from Librispeech to train DNN-HMM ASR and 460 clean data for i-vector extractor. To avoid overfitting, the dimensionality of i-vector is set as 100. We also tried larger i-vector dimensions but the i-vector with larger dimensions show similar performance compared to the i-vector system with size 100 dimensionality.

3.2.2 Phoneme Level Features

The phoneme related information have also been applied in emotion recognition system. Phoneme-dependent hidden Markov model (HMM) was proposed for emotion recognition system in (Lee et al., 2004). (Bitouk et al., 2010) proposed to extract class-level spectral features on three types of phoneme. Unlike most other work that need accurate alignment, we propose to use the statistics of posterior probability of phoneme on utterance level. The following steps are used to extract phoneme level features:

- Step One: Each frame x_t^u in utterance u is been feed into DNN pre-trained for ASR. The output is a numeric vector consisting of $p(s_i|x_t^u, DNN)$, which corresponding to posterior probability of triphone state s_i. The number of triphone state is dependent on the decision tree algorithm in the ASR system.

- Step Two: Mapping the tri-phone state s_i

into monophone. The number of the triphone state is huge. For emotion recognition system, it is not necessary to know information in such fine-grained unit. Instead, we map the triphone state into monophone level by disregarding left and right phone in the triphone structure. The mapping function is: $F_{map}(s_i) = m_j$ where s_i is the tri-phone state and m_j represents corresponding monophone. For example, $F_{map}(r - ae - n) = ae$.

- Step Three: Calculating the statistics of posterior probability of phoneme on utterance level. Given x_t^u, for each cluster m_j, we sum up the posterior probability $p(s_i|x_t^u, DNN)$ once s_i belongs to cluster m_j.

$$P_{m_j}(x_t^u) = \sum_{F_{map}(s_i)=m_j} p(s_i|x_t^u, DNN)$$

(2)

It generates a vector in the length of number of monophone for each frame in utterance u. In order to obtain a fixed dimensional feature for each utterance with variable length, statistics functionals, mean and standard deviation are applied on $P_M(X)$.

For each utterance, the generated feature set is a fixed dimensional vector. Based on the trained DNN-HMM ASR system, the number of tri-phone states and monophone ends up in 5672 and 58 respectively. After mapping and feature extraction, the dimensionality of the phoneme level features is 106.

4 Network Architectures

The models described here are based on a recurrent architecture and use different fusion strategies such as concatenation or tensor fusion across all modalities as well as across all segments of the video. We have integrated ideas from the two distinct approaches to jointly leverage multimodal fusion across modalities and across temporal segments and developed our Multimodal Relational Tensor Network.

4.1 Tensor Fusion Network

TFN consists of a Tensor Fusion Layer that explicitly models the unimodal, bimodal and trimodal inter-modal interactions using a 3-fold Cartesian product from modality embeddings. Most common deep learning approach for fusion of signals is a algebraic Merge operation where the operators are generally a linear concatenation of features or a sum. TFN, on the other hand, tries to disentangle unimodal, bimodal and trimodal dynamics by modeling each of them explicitly. Tensor Fusion is defined as the three-fold Cartesian product amongst the modalities with an extra constant '1' added to the dimension. The extra constant dimension with value '1' analytically generates all the multimodal dynamics followed with vector dot operations. This definition is mathematically equivalent to a differentiable outer product between the modalities. This operation results is a very large number of dimensions in the merged layer and therefore can realistically be applied to problems where the interaction space is not too large.

4.2 Contextual LSTM

Utterances in a video maintain a continuous sequence and work like state machines following a certain path before changing courses. Statistical Sequence classification techniques are applied in the classification of each member of the sequence by modeling the dependence on the other members of the sequence. Human reactions are also generally continuous and maintain a certain state in the sequence before jumping to another state. In particular, it has been seen that, when classifying one utterance, other utterances can provide important contextual information. This natural phenomenon directly maps to methods such as recurrent network approaches and sequence models to capture the dependencies between the segments. We reuse this idea to capture this flow of informational triggers across utterances using an LSTM-based recurrent neural network (RNN).

4.3 Relational Tensor Network

While TFN has been used to model the modality interactions within a video segment, we extend that approach to apply it to the contextual stream of segments. There are two ways we can apply a tensor fusion (by tensor fusion, we specifically refer to the cartesian product operation between the modalities with an extra '1' input to model the inter-modal interaction) across modalities across the streams. The first approach is to apply a tensor fusion across all modality features of all segments for all the modalities. This approach ideally captures all possible cross-dynamics (unimodal, bimodal, trimodal) amongst all possible features of all the video segments. The main issue with this

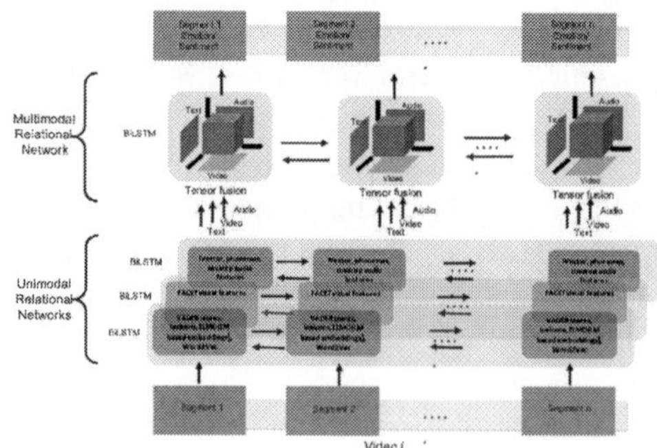

Figure 2: Relational Tensor Network

approach is that we run into an exponential growth in the feature space with every modality added in the interaction. The cartesian product further creates multiple outer products for bimodal and trimodal interactions. Even with a small number of features for this approach, our network had about 10s of billions of parameters and this would not be a feasible approach unless deployed on a massive infrastructure. This approach does not require the use of LSTMs as used in the Contextual LSTM work to capture the sequence information in the segments.

The other more feasible approach is to apply tensor fusion across modality features of each segment and then model the sequential interactions between the segments of the video using an LSTM Network. We depict our network in Figure 2.

This approach allows generation of contextually rich features that learn their weights not only from the current rich multimodal interactions but also leveraging previous interactions in the process. For example, interactions amongst audio and text features together can have a multiplicative effect to recognize certain kinds of emotion better (for example, high arousal negative words multiplied together can show stronger bias for the angry emotion). Also, these interactions persist across the segments and can help generate more meaningful recognizer of multimodal interactions. The intuitive explanation of this network is that it captures the long term multiplicative effects of interactions across segments for unimodal, bimodal and trimodal features. Neither the TFN model or the contextual model alone can effectively capture these interactions in principle.

Baseline	Binary		7-class		Regression
	Acc	F1	Acc	F1	MAE
$SVM\ multimodal$	60.4	0.61	23.5	0.27	1.38
$LSTM\_uni\_audio$	58	0.52	41	0.37	0.73
$LSTM\_uni\_video$	57.9	0.51	45.9	0.40	0.68
$LSTM\_uni\_text$	64.2	0.60	45.8	0.43	0.618
$LSTM\_earlyfusion$	65.2	0.62	46.6	0.44	0.60
TFN	66	0.62	47.9	0.43	0.58
RTN	**66.8**	**0.63**	**49.17**	**0.45**	**0.58**

Table 1: Sentiment Analysis Model Results

5 Experiments

We present multiple sets of experiments in order to evaluate the different models, impact of textual and audio features on sentiment and emotion prediction. Our training data consists of CMU-MOSEI training set where we do a 90/10 split for validation and early stopping experiments. All our results in this paper are reported on the CMU-MOSEI validation set[1].

5.1 Architecture comparisons

Table 1 and Table 2 show the performance of the various models on sentiment and emotion classification. We have used three LSTM based unimodal baselines, each for audio, video and text modalities. From the table, we see that unimodal-text network outperforms both audio and video modalities for sentiment. Unimodal-text also outperforms SVM multimodal for sentiment analysis, which is an SVM model trained on concatenated features from all the three modalities. The early fusion network is an LSTM based network(an extension of the unimodal networks),that takes in concatenated features from the three modalities. This LSTM model outperforms the SVM multimodal baseline by almost 5% binary class accuracy scores for sentiment analysis. All of these LSTM based networks outperform SVM by a huge margin in the 7-class classification scores and MAE for sentiment analysis. The TFN network with rich set of textual features slightly outperforms the simple concatenation technique(early fusion model) for sentiment and emotion recognition. The model with the best performance is the Relational Tensor Network model for both sentiment and emotion recognition that considers the neighboring tensor fusion networks for a given segment.

---

[1]The test set was not released at the time of writing.

5.2 Ablation study

Table 3 shows the detailed ablation study of the various text features that we have used in our models. We added word based features using lexicons and language model based ELMo embeddings and utterance level sentiment scores using VADER scores. As the table shows, adding lexicons result in a slight drop in performance of the scores. The lexicons we've used are extremely sparse compared to the vocabulary space of Word Vectors. Also we've simplistically concatenated the binary scores for Positive and and Negative category words to the same embeddings space as for the word vectors. Majority of these values remain 0 after the operation. We are exploring other ways to leverage the lexicon embeddings to allow a larger contribution of these signals to the classification process. Addition of the ELMo embeddings improves the performance as compared to using word embeddings alone. Addition of ELMo embeddings and segment level sentiment scores using Vader gives the best performance for binary, 7-class and MAE scores, as compared to adding individual features, or a combination of features. As described in ELMo work, adding the layers at different positions of the network helps to abstract various naturally occurring syntactic and semantic information about the words. For the audio modality, we presented two additional featuresets in the previous section, i-vector features and phoneme level features alongwith COVAREP features. Based on our experiments, we observed that the performance of the Emotion recognition RTN model with all these features were similar but improved slightly for 'Happy' emotion compared to the RTN model without the additional audio features.

6 Conclusion

In this paper we present a novel model called Relational Tensor Network for multimodal Affect Recognition that takes into account the context of a segment in a video based on the relations and interactions with its neighboring segments within the video. We meticulously add various feature set on the word level, that involves language model based embeddings and segment level sentiment features. Our model shows the best performance as compared to the state of the art techniques for sentiment and emotion recognition on the CMU-MOSEI dataset.

	Anger	Disgust	Fear	Happy	Sad	Surprise
SVM multimodal	0.358	0.19	0.21	1.167	0.33	0.171
LSTM_uni_audio	0.17	0.079	0.09	0.475	0.20	0.073
LSTM_uni_text	0.16	0.08	0.086	0.485	0.195	0.068
LSTM_uni_video	0.148	0.08	0.10	0.42	0.208	0.076
LSTM_earlyfusion	0.148	0.078	0.09	0.428	0.19	0.073
TFN	0.147	0.07	0.089	0.466	0.1766	0.074
RTN	**0.137**	**0.065**	**0.072**	**0.422**	**0.176**	**0.059**

Table 2: Emotion Recognition Model Results - MAE scores

Baseline	Binary		7-class		Regression
	Acc	F1	Acc	F1	MAE
Embedding only	64.6	0.60	48.17	0.43	0.595
Emb + Lex	62.8	0.57	45.6	0.41	0.61
Emb + Vader	64.2	0.59	45.4	0.42	0.61
Emb + ELMO	65.5	0.61	47.5	0.44	0.589
Emb + Lex + Vader	64.2	0.59	47.5	0.44	0.59
Emb + ELMO + Lex	64.6	0.58	48.7	0.45	0.576
Emb + ELMO + Vader	**66.4**	**0.63**	**48.9**	**0.44**	**0.577**
All features	66	0.62	47.9	0.43	0.58

Table 3: Text Ablation Study

References

T. Baltruaitis, P. Robinson, and L. P. Morency. 2016. Openface: An open source facial behavior analysis toolkit. In *2016 IEEE Winter Conference on Applications of Computer Vision (WACV)*, pages 1–10.

Dmitri Bitouk, Ragini Verma, and Ani Nenkova. 2010. Class-level spectral features for emotion recognition. *Speech communication*, 52(7-8):613–625.

G. Degottex, J. Kane, T. Drugman, T. Raitio, and S. Scherer. 2014. Covarep x2014; a collaborative voice analysis repository for speech technologies. In *2014 IEEE International Conference on Acoustics, Speech and Signal Processing (ICASSP)*, pages 960–964.

Abhinav Dhall, Roland Goecke, Jyoti Joshi, Michael Wagner, and Tom Gedeon. 2013. Emotion recognition in the wild challenge 2013. In *Proceedings of the 15th ACM on International conference on multimodal interaction*, pages 509–516. ACM.

P. EKMAN. 2002. Facial action coding system (facs). *A Human Face*.

Paul Ekman. 2009. *Telling Lies: Clues to Deceit in the Marketplace, Politics, and Marriage (Revised Edition)*. WW Norton & Company.

Dan Gusfield. 1997. *Algorithms on Strings, Trees and Sequences*. Cambridge University Press, Cambridge, UK.

Clayton J. Hutto and Eric Gilbert. 2014. Vader: A parsimonious rule-based model for sentiment analysis of social media text. In *ICWSM*. The AAAI Press.

Lakshmish Kaushik, Abhijeet Sangwan, and John HL Hansen. 2013. Sentiment extraction from natural audio streams. In *Acoustics, Speech and Signal Processing (ICASSP), 2013 IEEE International Conference on*, pages 8485–8489. IEEE.

Chul Min Lee, Serdar Yildirim, Murtaza Bulut, Abe Kazemzadeh, Carlos Busso, Zhigang Deng, Sungbok Lee, and Shrikanth Narayanan. 2004. Emotion recognition based on phoneme classes. In *Eighth International Conference on Spoken Language Processing*.

Yun Lei, Nicolas Scheffer, Luciana Ferrer, and Mitchell McLaren. 2014. A novel scheme for speaker recognition using a phonetically-aware deep neural network. In *Acoustics, Speech and Signal Processing (ICASSP), 2014 IEEE International Conference on*, pages 1695–1699. IEEE.

Bing Liu. 2010. Sentiment analysis and subjectivity. *Handbook of natural language processing*, 2:627–666.

Bryan McCann, James Bradbury, Caiming Xiong, and Richard Socher. 2017. Learned in translation: Contextualized word vectors.

Michael Neumann and Ngoc Thang Vu. 2017. Attentive convolutional neural network based speech emotion recognition: A study on the impact of input features, signal length, and acted speech. *arXiv preprint arXiv:1706.00612*.

Vassil Panayotov, Guoguo Chen, Daniel Povey, and Sanjeev Khudanpur. 2015. Librispeech: an asr corpus based on public domain audio books. In *Acoustics, Speech and Signal Processing (ICASSP), 2015 IEEE International Conference on*, pages 5206–5210. IEEE.

Bo Pang and Lillian Lee. 2008. Opinion mining and sentiment analysis. *Foundations and trends in information retrieval*, 2(1-2):1–135.

Jeffrey Pennington, Richard Socher, and Christopher D. Manning. 2014. Glove: Global vectors for word representation. In *Empirical Methods in Natural Language Processing (EMNLP)*, pages 1532–1543.

Matthew E. Peters, Mark Neumann, Mohit Iyyer, Matthew Gardner, Christopher Clark, Kenton Lee, and Luke S. Zettlemoyer. 2018. Deep contextualized word representations. *CoRR*, abs/1802.05365.

Robert Plutchik. 2001. The nature of emotions human emotions have deep evolutionary roots, a fact that may explain their complexity and provide tools for clinical practice. *American Scientist*.

Soujanya Poria, Erik Cambria, Devamanyu Hazarika, Navonil Majumder, Amir Zadeh, and Louis-Philippe Morency. 2017. Context-dependent sentiment analysis in user-generated videos. In *ACL*.

Jonathan Posner, James A Russell, and Bradley S Peterson. 2005. The circumplex model of affect: An integrative approach to affective neuroscience, cognitive development, and psychopathology. *Development and psychopathology*, 17(03):715–734.

Daniel Povey, Arnab Ghoshal, Gilles Boulianne, Lukas Burget, Ondrej Glembek, Nagendra Goel, Mirko Hannemann, Petr Motlicek, Yanmin Qian, Petr Schwarz, et al. 2011. The kaldi speech recognition toolkit. In *IEEE 2011 workshop on automatic speech recognition and understanding*, EPFL-CONF-192584. IEEE Signal Processing Society.

Klaus R Scherer. 1984. Emotion as a multicomponent process: A model and some cross-cultural data. *Review of Personality & Social Psychology*.

Björn W Schuller, Stefan Steidl, Anton Batliner, Julia Hirschberg, Judee K Burgoon, Alice Baird, Aaron C Elkins, Yue Zhang, Eduardo Coutinho, and Keelan Evanini. 2016. The interspeech 2016 computational paralinguistics challenge: Deception, sincerity & native language. In *Interspeech*, pages 2001–2005.

Bonggun Shin, Timothy Lee, and Jinho D. Choi. 2017. Lexicon integrated cnn models with attention for sentiment analysis. In *WASSA@EMNLP*.

Philip J Stone, Dexter C Dunphy, and Marshall S Smith. 1966. The general inquirer: A computer approach to content analysis.

Fei Tao and Gang Liu. 2017. Advanced lstm: A study about better time dependency modeling in emotion recognition. *arXiv preprint arXiv:1710.10197*.

Fei Tao, Gang Liu, and Qingen Zhao. 2018. An ensemble framework of voice-based emotion recognition system for films and tv programs. *arXiv preprint arXiv:1803.01122*.

Michel Valstar, Jonathan Gratch, Björn Schuller, Fabien Ringeval, Denis Lalanne, Mercedes Torres Torres, Stefan Scherer, Giota Stratou, Roddy Cowie, and Maja Pantic. 2016. Avec 2016: Depression, mood, and emotion recognition workshop and challenge. In *Proceedings of the 6th International Workshop on Audio/Visual Emotion Challenge*, pages 3–10. ACM.

Rui Xia and Yang Liu. 2016. Dbn-ivector framework for acoustic emotion recognition. In *INTERSPEECH*, pages 480–484.

A Zadeh, PP Liang, S Poria, P Vij, E Cambria, and LP Morency. 2018a. Multi-attention recurrent network for human communication comprehension. In *AAAI*.

Amir Zadeh, Minghai Chen, Soujanya Poria, Erik Cambria, and Louis-Philippe Morency. 2017. Tensor fusion network for multimodal sentiment analysis. *CoRR*, abs/1707.07250.

Amir Zadeh, Paul Pu Liang, Navonil Mazumder, Soujanya Poria, Erik Cambria, and Louis-Philippe Morency. 2018b. Memory fusion network for multi-view sequential learning. *arXiv preprint arXiv:1802.00927*.

Amir Zadeh, Paul Pu Liang, Soujanya Poria, Erik Cambria, and Louis-Philippe Morency. 2018c. Human multimodal language in the wild: A novel dataset and interpretable dynamic fusion model. *Association for Computational Linguistics*.

Amir Zadeh, Paul Pu Liang, Jon Vanbriesen, Soujanya Poria, Erik Cambria, Minghai Chen, and Louis-Philippe Morency. 2018d. Multimodal language analysis in the wild: Cmu-mosei dataset and interpretable dynamic fusion graph. In *Association for Computational Linguistics (ACL)*.

Convolutional Attention Networks for Multimodal Emotion Recognition from Speech and Text Data

Chan Woo Lee[1], Kyu Ye Song[1], Jihoon Jeong[2], Woo Yong Choi[1]*

[1]orbis.ai Inc., Seoul, South Korea
[1]{cwlee, kysong, cchoi}@orbisai.co
[2]Kyung Hee Cyber University, South Korea
[2]jjeong@khcu.ac.kr

Abstract

Emotion recognition has become a popular topic of interest, especially in the field of human computer interaction. Previous works involve unimodal analysis of emotion, while recent efforts focus on multimodal emotion recognition from vision and speech. In this paper, we propose a new method of learning about the hidden representations between just speech and text data using convolutional attention networks. Compared to the shallow model which employs simple concatenation of feature vectors, the proposed attention model performs much better in classifying emotion from speech and text data contained in the CMU-MOSEI dataset.

1 Introduction

Emotion not only is a key driver to people's actions and thoughts, but also is a fundamental part of human communication. As such, emotion recognition technology has become growingly important in improving how humans interact with machines [1]. For instance, emotion recognition has been applied to analyze people's reactions to advertisements, thus creating better neuromarketing campaigns [2]. It has also gained in popularity amongst various other domains such as healthcare [3], customer service, or gaming.

However, effective emotion recognition still remains a challenging task, due to the sheer complexity of generalizing human emotions. For

---

* Corresponding Author: cchoi@orbisai.co

example, individuals express and perceive emotions differently, depending on numerous personal characteristics such as but not limited to age [4], gender [5] and race. Previous efforts have used deep learning based approaches to analyze emotion from single mode of expression, such as facial expression [6] or speech [7]. Since deep learning based approaches have been proven to be effective at learning and generalizing data with high-dimensional feature spaces like images, similar efforts to capture complex feature space of emotional data have also shown promising results with several emotion databases such as EmoDB [8] or IEMOCAP [9]. Unfortunately, human emotion in real-life is often expressed through complex combination of multiple modes of expression, and a lot of information is lost by employing unimodal analysis.

To solve this problem, using deep learning based approaches for multimodal emotion recognition has been researched extensively in recent years. Work of Tzirakis *et al.* uses deep residual networks to extract features from facial expressions, convolutional neural networks to extract features from speech, and concatenates them to input into a LSTM network [10]. Work of Ranganathan *et al.* uses deep believe networks on facial expressions, body expressions, vocal expressions, and physiological signals [11].

Inspired by these approaches, we suggest a new approach to multimodal emotion recognition from just speech and text data. Feature vectors from embedded text sequences and speech spectrograms are extracted using convolutional neural network based architectures. A direct way to learn about the relationship between these two

Proceedings of the First Grand Challenge and Workshop on Human Multimodal Language (Challenge-HML), pages 28–34,
Melbourne, Australia July 20, 2018. ©2018 Association for Computational Linguistics

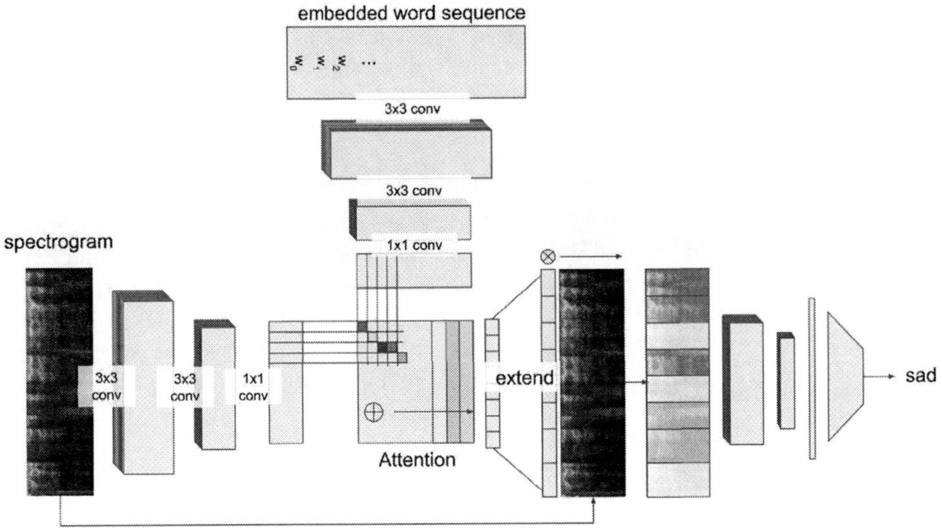

Figure 1 Attention Networks for multimodal representation learning between speech and text data for emotion classification. Separate CNNs are used to extract features from speech spectrograms and embedded word sequences. An attention matrix of m x n dimension is calculated by simply taking a softmax of the dot products of the feature vectors. This attention matrix is then multiplied to the spectrogram input, and goes through a third CNN for emotion classification.

feature vectors would be to utilize a *shallow model*, which is a simple concatenation of two feature vectors. However, since the correlations between feature vectors from speech and text is highly non-linear, it is difficult for a shallow model to properly learn multimodal representations. Therefore, we utilize trainable attention mechanisms to learn nonlinear correlations between these feature vectors. Attention mechanisms also help retain information in the time-domain by forming temporal embedding between two feature vectors. Since speech features and context shares the same time domain, using attention mechanism may help to discover new information for emotion classification. Attention models have previously been successfully applied to tasks such as image caption generation [12], machine translation [13], and speech recognition [14].

To demonstrate the benefits of this new approach, we use it to classify emotions from speech and text data provided in the CMU-MOSEI dataset into six classes: happy, angry, sad, surprised, disgusted, and fear [15]. We also compare this approach to the shallow model approach to show how the attention mechanism can improve capturing of multimodal correlations between text and speech.

2 Model

The attention network shown in figure 1 is comprised of three separate convolutional neural networks: one each for feature extraction from speech spectrogram and word embedding sequence, and one for emotion classifier. Outputs from each of the CNNs from word embedding and spectrogram are used to compute an attention matrix for representing word embedding's correlation to the spectrogram with respect to the emotion labelling. This attention matrix combined with the input spectrogram to be inputted into the CNN based classifier for emotion.

Input embedded word sequences have a size of $R^{e \times L}$ (e: embedding size, L: max sequence length), while input spectrograms have a size of $R^{f \times t}$ (f: frequency range, t: time domain after FT). Word embedding size is fixed at 300, and raw text sentence length was capped at 40 words. Thereby, total word embedding sequence dimension results to 300 by 40. Input spectrograms are derived from transforming raw audio signals with a sample rate of 8000 Hz in the frequency ranges of 0~4kHz, with a fixed size of 200 x 400.

To find the attention matrix between the two feature vectors, 1 by 1 convolution is conducted before calculating the dot product. The resulting attention matrix has a size of m x n, determined by the last feature vector after 1 by 1 convolution. The column of the attention matrix is the attention of word sequence with respect to the spatial distribution of the input spectrogram. At the extend stage, feature dimensions that are lost due to max pooling in the convolutional layers is recovered. By broadcasting attention values by 2^P, where P is the number of max pooling layers applied, attention values applied to the entire width of the spectrogram.

Attention values are calculated using the following equations:

$$a_{it} = \frac{exp(e_i \cdot f_t)}{\Sigma_{t=1}^{T} \exp(e_t \cdot f_t)} \qquad (1)$$

$$c_t = \sum_{t=1}^{m} a_{it} f_t \qquad (2)$$

e_i stands for the word embedded latent vector, while f_t stands for the spectrogram latent vector. By taking a dot product of e_i and f_t and taking a softmax of it, we are able to calculate a_{it}. Since taking a dot product of e_i and f_t essentially equates to calculating the similarity between to vectors, a_{it} is the similarity distribution with respect to time domain. Next, by multiplying a_{it} and f_t element-wise, c_t can be obtained, which essentially is the input spectrogram with attention information added. As shown in Figure 1, the attention matrix can be constructed with m x n dimensions, and when visualized looks like Figure 2.

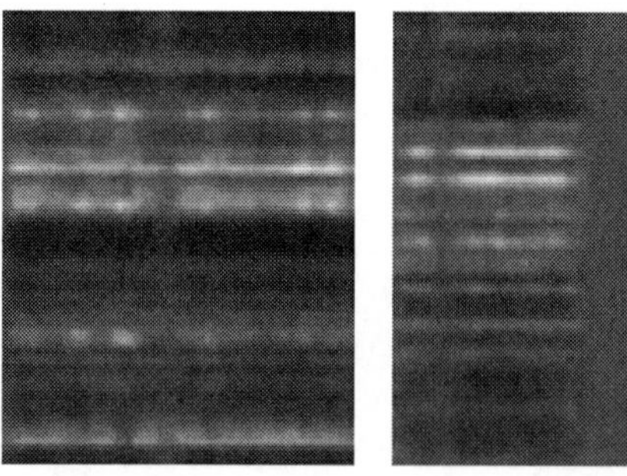

Figure 2 Visualization of the attention matrix. Row means time domain matching the input spectrogram, column means word sequence

After the model learns the representation of each features for attention, the last CNN layer computes the weighted sum of all the information extracted from the attention input. The output vector is then fed into a fully connected softmax layer for classification.

3 Data and preprocessing

3.1 Dataset

We use audio and text data from CMU-Multimodal Opinion Sentiment and Emotion Intensity (CMU-MOSEI) dataset for all experiments [15]. The videos, totaling 23,141 files, are chosen from YouTube speakers including various topics and monologue, and are gender balanced.

Annotations consist of six emotion indexes: sadness (2843), angry (6794), happy (10028), disgust (1845), surprise (349), fear (817) with value ranges of [0,4.6], and sentiment label with a value range of [-3,3]. The dataset is organized by video IDs and corresponding segments with six emotion and sentiment labels. Video IDs are then further split into segments. The training set consists 3303 video ID and 23453 segments, while the validation set consists of non-overlapping 300 video IDs and 1834 segments.

Text embedding was prepared using GloVe word2vec method. Each word embedding is fixed at a length of 300. The duration of each word utterance is also provided by the P2FA forced alignment [15].

3.2 Data preprocessing

Speech raw signals are converted to spectrograms before being input into the attention network using Short Time Fourier Transform (STFT) after resampling with a reduced sample rate from 44100 Hz to 8000Hz, as seen in Figure 3. Hamming window is used during STFT, and the length of each segment is 800. The transformed spectrogram is then converted to log-scale to make the vertical axis units of dB, with a frame size of 200x400.

4 Experimental results

In this section, we describe the experiment methodologies and report the recognition performance proposed attention network architecture on the CMU-MOSEI dataset [15].

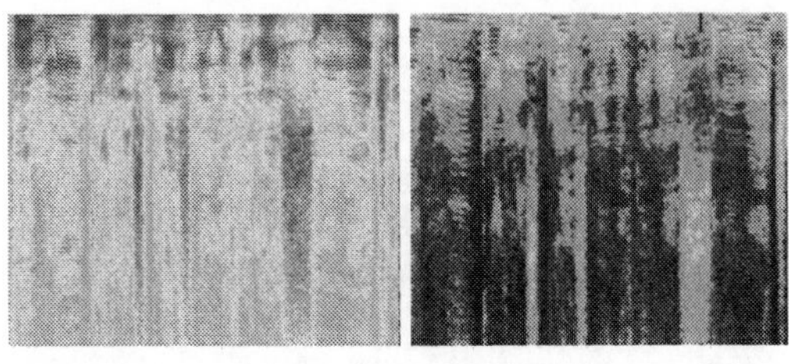

Figure 3 Speech spectrogram after STFT (Left: after STFT, Right: log scale)

4.1 Methods

All models are trained with the training dataset provided by the ACL 2018 Multimodal Challenge. This training dataset is a subset of the entire CMU-MOSEI dataset. The models are validated using the provided validation dataset, again as part of the Challenge. Two sets of experiments are conducted: First, the shallow model architecture (Figure 3) is trained with the training set. The proposed attention network architecture is trained end-to-end, and validated for performance. We then train a shallow model as outlined in Figure 3 to use as a baseline to track how much improvement the attention network provides in learning the correlation between word embedding and corresponding spectrogram features.

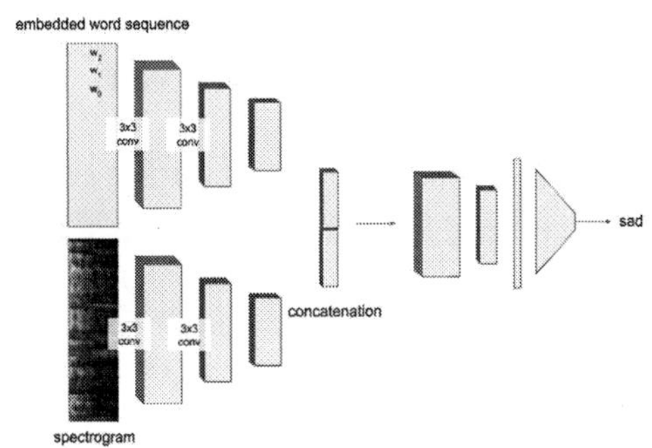

Figure 4 Shallow model diagram

4.2 Hyperparameters

Stochastic gradient descent with a set learning rate is employed during training. For regularization, dropout is applied to the last hidden layer. The system's hyperparameters are: 32 kernels with 3 kernel size; a batch size of 32; a dropout rate of 0.1; learning rate of 1e-3; a pool size of 2 and stride of 2; the dense layer units after final CNN are 1024, 512, and 128 for all configurations.

4.3 Evaluation

For each experiment, we report an overall accuracy (each sentence across the dataset has an equal weight; weighted accuracy) and a class accuracy (first evaluated for each emotion and then averaged; unweighted accuracy). All the classification results are listed in Tables 1-2, including precision, recall, and f-1 score. Confusion matrices are also provided to show how well the model correctly classifies each emotion, using the top-1 class prediction as a metric.

4.4 Experiment 1: shallow model

In this section, we report the results of training the shallow model with the CMU-MOSEI dataset. Since the shallow model is a common and the simplest method of multimodal emotion classification, we use it as a baseline for comparison.

The overall validation accuracy (weighted) is 83.11% and class validation accuracy (unweighted) is 77.23% as shown in Table 1. The multi-class confusion matrix is shown in Figure 5, showing the highest accuracies for anger and happy emotions, and lowest accuracies for fear and surprise emotions.

Emotion	Precision	Recall	f-1 score
sadness	0.82	0.65	0.73
happy	0.93	0.88	0.91
anger	0.75	0.90	0.82
disgust	0.75	0.75	0.75
surprise	0.98	0.55	0.70
fear	0.83	0.63	0.72
average	0.85	0.84	0.84
class accuracy	77.23%	Overall accuracy	83.11%

Table 1 The results of shallow model

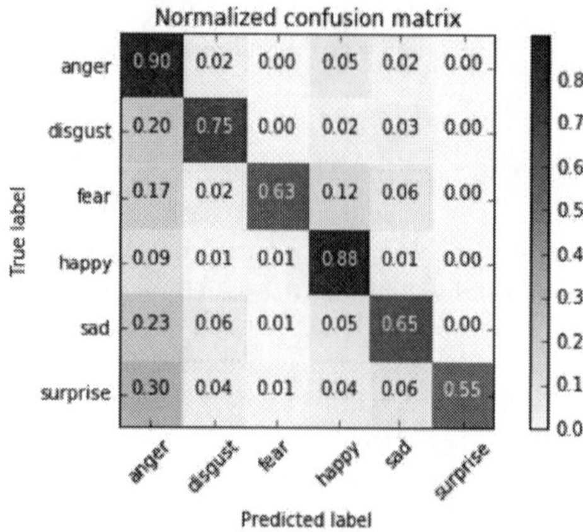

Figure 5 Confusion matrix of shallow model

4.5 Experiment 2: attention model

In this section, we report the results of attention model to compare to the baseline results.

The overall accuracy (weighted) is 88.89% and class accuracy (unweighted) is 84.08 % as shown in Table 2 for the attention model, a significant improvement from the same metrics of shallow model. According to the confusion matrix shown in Figure 6, validation accuracies have increased throughout all emotion classes compared to the baseline.

Emotion	Precision	Recall	f-1 score
sadness	0.88	0.86	0.87
happy	0.92	0.92	0.92
anger	0.85	0.92	0.88
disgust	0.88	0.81	0.84
surprise	0.98	0.62	0.76
fear	0.94	0.65	0.77
average	0.89	0.89	0.89
class accuracy	84.08%	Overall accuracy	88.89%

Table 2 The results of attention model

5 Discussion

Comparing the attention model to the shallow model, shallow model utilizes a superficial feature concatenation, while attention model calculates the similarity between two feature vectors that can be trained with learnable weights. In the context of the feature space, concatenating two feature vectors in the shallow model essentially is a simple increase in dimensionality. On the other hand, the feature space in the attention model is fixed to the audio feature space. However, since the features now depend on a new variable called attention, the model can selectively utilize different features in the audio feature space to different extents for better classification. In other words, text data now plays an important role in determining whether a speech feature is important or not in classifying certain emotions, an especially important benefit for training datasets with limited size or data balance.

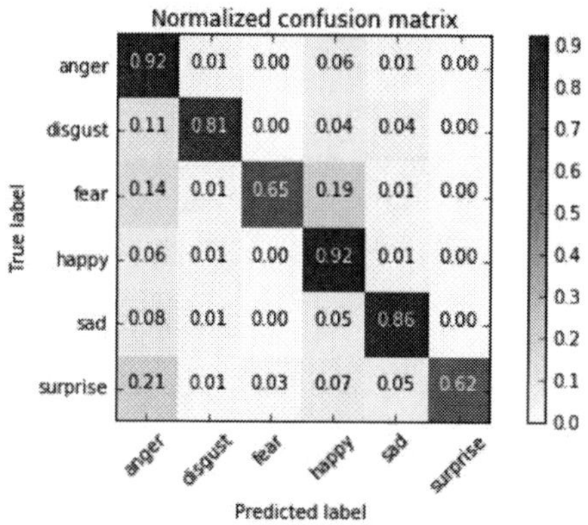

Figure 6 Confusion matrix of attention model

In addition, correlation information between text and speech with respect to the time domain can be easily lost when shallow concatenation is utilized. Meanwhile, calculation of the attention matrix requires matrix multiplication between embedded word and spectrogram feature for a given time. Hence, time series information is retained in the calculated attention matrix through temporal embedding, and to the resulting attention applied spectrogram. Since context and its vocal style of delivery plays an important role in communicating emotion, retaining the time information provides huge benefits in classifying emotions from just speech and text.

Furthermore, while the shallow model is merely an analysis of a union of text and speech information, the proposed attention model aims to discover new meaningful methods of how two feature vectors intersect. In other words, shallow model is highly single feature dependent, while attention model is not. This means that if each of the feature vectors contain inadequate information to begin with, shallow model will perform much worse than attention model.

Since the attention model provides newly discovered correlation between the two feature vectors, this new information can be used in ensemble with the original text and speech feature vectors.

Of course, attention models aren't silver bullets in choosing the desired features and discarding the rest. Without careful training of the model, distribution of the attention values can flatten out. For instance, if the input data contains too much padding, and the network has a big bias causing little optimization, the feature vector used to calculate the attention values will approximate to 0, and subsequently attention values will also approximate to 0. One possible solution is the utilize loss masking on the padding of the input data so that a more dynamic softmax distribution in the attention matrix can be obtained.

It is worth noting that for both experiments, f-1 scores of select classes, namely happy and anger are much higher than those of other classes. This is mainly due to a considerable class imbalance of the training set, in which ~44% of the data is happy, and ~30% of the data is angry.

6   Conclusion

The attention model proposed for multimodal emotion recognition from speech and text data provides an effective method of learning about the correlation between the two output feature vectors from separate yet jointly trained CNNs. This method is especially effective for correlation information between speech and text, because the context and the way it is delivered plays a crucial role in affective communication, and the attention model retains temporal information well throughout its model. For future work, syncing the input text and speech data in the temporal dimension may help the attention network focus on learning the relationship between one speech segment and one word, instead of the relationship between whole speech segment and whole text segment.

References

[1] Arkin, R. C.; Fujita, M.; Takagi, T.; and Hasegawa, R. 2003. An ethological and emotional basis for human–robot interaction. Robotics and Autonomous Systems 42(3):191–201.

[2] F.Burkhardt, J.Ajmera, R.Englert, J.Stegmann, and W.Burleson, "Detecting anger in automated voice portal dialogs," in Proc. Annu. Conf. Int. Speech Commun. Assoc., 2006, pp. 1053–1056.

[3] Q.Ji, Z.Zhu, and P.Lan, "Real-time non intrusive monitoring and prediction of driver fatigue," IEEE Trans. Veh. Technol., vol. 53, no. 4, pp. 1052– 1068, Jul. 2004.

[4] A.Mill, J.Alliketal.,"Age-related differences in emotion recognition ability: a cross-sectional study." Emotion, vol. 9, no. 5, p.619, 2009.

[5] T.Vogtand, E.Andre´, "Improving automatic emotion recognition from speech via gender differentiation," in Proc. Language Re-sources and Evaluation Conference (LREC 2006), Genoa, 2006.

[6] Simonyan, Karen, and Andrew Zisserman. "Very deep convolutional networks for large-scale image recognition." arXiv preprint arXiv:1409.1556 (2014).

[7] C.N.Anagnostopoulos, T.Iliou, andI. Giannoukos, "Features and classifiers for emotion recognition from speech : A survey from 2000 to 2011," Artif. Intell. Rev., vol. 43, no. 2, pp. 155– 177, 2015.

[8] Burkhardt, F., Paeschke, A., Rolfes, M., Sendlmeier, W., and Weiss, B. A database of german emotional speech. In Proc. INTERSPEECH 2005, Lissabon, Portugal (2005), pp. 1517–1520.

[9] Busso, Carlos, et al. "IEMOCAP: Interactive emotional dyadic motion capture database." Language resources and evaluation 42.4 (2008): 335

[10] Tzirakis, P., Trigeorgis, G., Nicolaou, M. A., Schuller, B. W., & Zafeiriou, S. (2017). End-to-end multimodal emotion recognition using deep neural networks. IEEE Journal of Selected Topics in Signal Processing, 11(8), 1301-1309.

[11] Ranganathan, H., Chakraborty, S., & Panchanathan, S. (2016, March). Multimodal emotion

recognition using deep learning architectures. In Applications of Computer Vision (WACV), 2016 IEEE Winter Conference on (pp. 1-9). IEEE.

[12] K. Xu, J. Ba, R. Kiros, K. Cho, A. C. Courville, R. Salakhutdinov,R. S. Zemel, and Y. Bengio, "Show, attend and tell: Neural image caption generation with visual attention." in ICML, vol. 14,2015,pp.77–81.

[13] D. Bahdanau, K. Cho, and Y. Bengio, "Neural machine translation by jointly learning to align and translate,"arXiv preprint arXiv: 1409.0473 2014

[14] J.K.Chorowski, D.Bahdanau, D.Serdyuk, K.Cho, and Y.Ben-gio, "Attention-based models for speech recognition," in Advances in Neural Information Processing Systems, 2015, pp. 577–585.

[15] Zadeh, Amir, et al. "Human Multimodal Language in the Wild: A Novel Dataset and Interpretable Dynamic Fusion Model" Association for Computational Linguistics (2018)

[16] Poria, Soujanya, et al. "Context-dependent sentiment analysis in user-generated videos" Proceedings of the 55th Annual Meeting of the Association for Computational Linguistics (Volume 1: Long Papers) pp. 873-883 (2017)

[17] Zadeh, Amir, et al. "Multi-attention recurrent network for human communication comprehension" arXiv preprint arXiv:1802.00923 (2018)

[18] Poria, S., Cambria, E., Hazarika, D., Majumder, N., Zadeh, A. and Morency, L.P., 2017. Context-dependent sentiment analysis in user-generated videos. In Proceedings of the 55th Annual Meeting of the Association for Computational Linguistics (Volume 1: Long Papers) (Vol. 1, pp. 873-883).

[19] Poria, S., Cambria, E., Hazarika, D., Mazumder, N., Zadeh, A. and Morency, L.P., 2017, November. Multi-level Multiple Attentions for Contextual Multimodal Sentiment Analysis. In 2017 IEEE International Conference on Data Mining (ICDM) (pp. 1033-1038). IEEE.

[20] Zadeh, A., Liang, P., Vanbriesen, J., Poria, S., Cambria, E., Chen, M., Morency, L., 2018. Multimodal Language Analysis in the Wild: CMU-MOSEI Dataset and Interpretable Dynamic Fusion Graph. Association for Computational Linguistics.

Sentiment Analysis using Imperfect Views from Spoken Language and Acoustic Modalities

Imran Sheikh, Sri Harsha Dumpala, Rupayan Chakraborty, Sunil Kumar Kopparapu
TCS Research and Innovations-Mumbai, INDIA
{imran.as, d.harsha, rupayan.chakraborty, sunilkumar.kopparapu}@tcs.com

Abstract

Multimodal sentiment classification in practical applications may have to rely on erroneous and imperfect views, namely (a) language transcription from a speech recognizer and (b) under-performing acoustic views. This work focuses on improving the representations of these views by performing a deep canonical correlation analysis with the representations of the better performing manual transcription view. Enhanced representations of the imperfect views can be obtained even in absence of the perfect views and give an improved performance during test conditions. Evaluations on the CMU-MOSI and CMU-MOSEI datasets demonstrate the effectiveness of the proposed approach.

1 Introduction

Use of multimodal cues is especially useful for analyzing sentiment in audio-visual data like opinion videos on social media websites, call-center audio recordings etc. The different modalities, viz. language (spoken words), acoustic (speech) and visual (facial and gestures), can carry a different view of the same information like for example, sentiment. While the representations/features extracted from these individual different views add richness to the sentiment classification, the intra and inter view-interactions play an important role in better sentiment classification (Zadeh et al., 2017; Chen et al., 2018; Rajagopalan et al., 2016; Nojavanasghari et al., 2016; Xu et al., 2013).

Although fusion of multi-view information is being extensively explored, the challenges associated with the presence of noise and irregularities in a view has received very less attention. For instance, multimodal sentiment classification systems have typically used manual, and hence, error free language transcriptions and exploited the interaction of other views with this noise free language view (Zadeh et al., 2018, 2017). However, a practical system will have to rely on a language transcription from an Automatic Speech Recognition (ASR) engine, which is inherently prone to errors due to ambient/channel noises in acoustic environments (Gong, 1995; Li et al., 2014), language domain mismatch, emotion in speech (Athanaselis et al., 2005), etc. Similarly, existing and popularly used representations of the acoustic view have generally under-performed compared to the language view (Poria et al., 2017; Zadeh et al., 2018; Pérez-Rosas et al., 2013), indicating that the acoustic view or its representations, by themselves, may not be discriminative enough for robust sentiment classification.

Assuming the ASR (language transcription) and acoustic views as imperfect views, the focus of this work is on improving the representations of these noisy views, riding on the representations of the better performing view. We show that the representations obtained from automatic transcriptions of spoken language and those from the acoustic views can be enhanced using corresponding representations from manual transcriptions of spoken language. Enhanced representations of the imperfect views can be obtained even in absence of the perfect views during test conditions. Deep canonical correlation analysis (DCCA) (Andrew et al., 2013) is used to improve the representations of the imperfect views. The rest of the paper is organized as follows. Section 2 describes a method to improve imperfect or erroneous views. Section 3 presents the different components in our multimodal sentiment classification system. Experiments are discussed in Section 4 followed by a discussion on results and conclusion in Section 5.

Proceedings of the First Grand Challenge and Workshop on Human Multimodal Language (Challenge-HML), pages 35–39,
Melbourne, Australia July 20, 2018. ©2018 Association for Computational Linguistics

2 Improving representations of spoken language and acoustic views

Multimodal sentiment classification works have mainly relied on the manual transcription of the spoken utterances. In a practical and real life scenario, the text transcriptions are not readily available and are required to be obtained from an ASR engine. While ASR systems have seen large improvements with the use of deep learning methods, their performance is impacted by mismatched train-test conditions. As a result, practical multimodal sentiment classification systems will have to rely on imperfect spoken language views.

On the other hand, acoustic views used by multimodal sentiment classification systems have shown poor performance compared to that of the language view. This might indicate that either the acoustic view or its utterance level audio representations are not discriminative enough for sentiment classification. Recent classification models capture interactions across view/modality and produce better sentiment classification results (Zadeh et al., 2018, 2017). In contrast to this, our work focuses on improving representations of the imperfect views using representations of the better performing view. Utterance level representations obtained from ASR view and the acoustic view are improved using the representations extracted from manual transcriptions of spoken language. These representation improvements are achieved using DCCA (Andrew et al., 2013).

2.1 Deep canonical correlation analysis

Given the representations of two different views of the same signal, DCCA learns a pair of non-linear transformations such that the transformed representations for the two views are maximally correlated. The individual transformed representations from a DCCA model have been shown to capture information from both the views and as a result outperform the original individual representations (Andrew et al., 2013; Wang et al., 2015; Shao et al., 2015). Figure 1 shows a high level block representation of DCCA. (f_{v1}, f_{v2}) are representations of two views of the same input data, nonlinear transformations are carried out using DNNs and canonical correlations are computed on the DNN transformed representations ($\hat{f}_{v1}$, $\hat{f}_{v2}$). During training, representations for the two views are extracted from the train set and used to train the DNN's such that canonical corre-

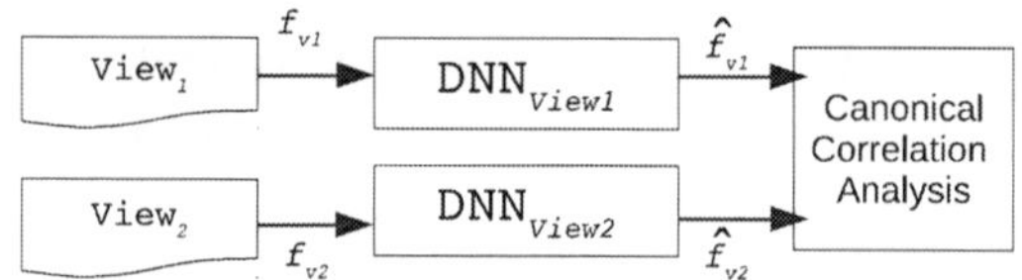

Figure 1: Improving views using DCCA.

lation between the transformed representations is maximized. Thus, the goal is to learn parameters W_1^*, W_2^* for DNN_{View1}, DNN_{View2}, such that:

$$(W_1^*, W_2^*) = \underset{W_1, W_2}{argmax} \; corr(g_1(f_{v1}; W_1),$$
$$g_2(f_{v2}; W_2))$$
$$\hat{f}_{v1} = g_1(f_{v1}; W_1) \;\;, \;\; \hat{f}_{v2} = g_2(f_{v2}; W_2)$$

where, g_1, g_2 denote the nonlinear transformations of DNN_{View1} and DNN_{View2} respectively. Once the DNNs are trained they are used to obtain the transformed or enhanced representations.

3 Sentiment classification using language and acoustic views

This section describes our complete system for sentiment classification which uses language and acoustic views. We first discuss the views and their representations and then describe the method adopted to fuse and classify these representations.

3.1 Spoken language views & representations

3.1.1 Manual and ASR views

A typical view of the spoken language modality is the word level manual transcription of the spoken utterances. However, in a realistic scenario manual transcriptions are not available and the system has to rely on automatic transcriptions of the spoken language. Therefore, we consider the automatic transcriptions from a general purpose ASR engine as a practical spoken language view.

To obtain the ASR view, we use the public domain Kaldi ASR toolkit (Povey et. al., 2011) along with the ASpIRE Chain acoustic models (Peddinti et al., 2015; Povey, 2017). The accompanying pre-trained language model is used as it is. When evaluated on the 2199 speech utterances in the CMU-MOSI dataset (Zadeh et al., 2016), this ASR setup gives a mean word error rate of 49.2% (with a standard deviation of 32.0). Its performance in terms of correctly recognized words is 66.8%.

3.1.2 CNN based representation

Representations for the spoken language views are obtained using a text convolutional neural network (CNN) (Kim, 2014). Each utterance is represented as the concatenation of 300-dimensional GloVe embeddings (Pennington et al., 2014). Then 1-dimensional convolution kernels are applied to the concatenated word embeddings. The CNN has two convolutional layers, with the first layer having two kernels of size 3 and 4 with 50 feature maps each and the second layer having a kernel of size 2 with 100 feature maps. Each convolutional layer was followed by a 2×2 max pooling layer. A fully connected layer transforms the CNN extracted features into a 300-dimensional vector.

3.2 Representation of acoustic view

As a representation of the acoustic view, we extract a large set of high level descriptors (HLDs) from low level audio descriptors (LLDs) like voice probability, MFCCs, pitch, RMS energies and their delta regression coefficients. Since the HLDs are (up to fourth order) statistics of LLDs extracted over smaller (20 ms) frames, the dimension of the acoustic features remain same (i.e. 384) for all utterances. We used the $IS09$ configuration from the openSMILE toolkit (Eyben et al., 2009).

3.3 Fusion and sentiment classification

Bi-modal representations for utterance level sentiment classification are obtained by first extracting the representations of (manually transcribed and ASR) spoken language views and those for the acoustic view, as discussed in Section 3.1. Then representations of automatically transcribed spoken language view and those for the acoustic view are improved using DCCA, as discussed in Section 2.1. Finally the improved representations are concatenated to obtain a bi-modal representation.

We use a bi-directional LSTM-RNN to label utterance level sentiments based on the bi-modal representations. Sequence labeling with LSTM-RNNs can account for contextual information from adjacent inputs as well as the overall input sequence and has been shown to perform better on several tasks (Graves and Schmidhuber, 2005; Graves et al., 2008; Poria et al., 2017; Sheikh et al., 2017). Let us denote the bi-modal representations as $(x_1, ...x_{t-1}, x_t, x_{t+1}..., x_N)$, where x_t represents the current utterance and N is the number of utterances in a video. We followed the hierarchical

training discussed in (Poria et al., 2017). Each bi-modal representation (x_t) is input to the forward and backward LSTM-RNNs to obtain the hidden layer activations h_t^F and h_t^B. These concatenated activations (c_t) are fed to softmax classifier,

$$p_t(i) = \frac{exp(c_{ti}.W_C + b_C)}{\sum_j exp(c_{tj}.W_C + b_C)} \qquad (1)$$

where $p_t(i)$ denotes the posterior probability of output class i for utterance at t; W_C and b_C are weight and bias parameters of the softmax layer.

4 Experiments and results

4.1 Datasets

We present our results and analysis on two datasets, namely, (a) CMU-MOSI (Zadeh et al., 2016) and (b) CMU-MOSEI (Zadeh, 2018a). CMU-MOSI consists of 93 movie related opinion videos from YouTube, segmented into 2199 clips/utterances. CMU-MOSEI consists of about 2500 multi-domain monologue videos from YouTube, segmented into $23,500$ clips/utterances.

Both CMU-MOSI and CMU-MOSEI datasets are annotated with utterance level sentiment labels in the range $[-3, 3]$. We focus on binary sentiment classification in which labels $[-3, 0]$ are considered as negative and $[1, 3]$ are considered as positive sentiments. For CMU-MOSI, we used the train, validation and test split provided by the CMU Multimodal Data SDK (Zadeh, 2018b). The SDK also provides a train, validation and test split for CMU-MOSEI. However, as the test set labels were not available at the time of submission of this paper, we treated 200 videos from the original validation set as our test set. The remaining 100 videos from the original validation set and an additional 150 videos from the original train set are considered as our validation set.

4.2 Experiment setup

We evaluate the performance of the spoken language and acoustic views, individually and in combination. The manual and ASR transcriptions of the language view are denoted as MT and AT, respectively. The acoustic view is denoted as AU. Enhanced (representations of) ASR view and acoustic view are denoted as AT$_\uparrow$ and AU$_\uparrow$, respectively. They were enhanced using (representations of) the manual transcription view, using the DCCA model described in Section 2.1. Our DCCA models use DNNs with 3 hidden layers and sigmoids.

4.3 Sentiment classification results

Table 1 presents the % accuracy (Acc.) and F-score (F1) for binary sentiment classification on the CMU-MOSI and CMU-MOSEI datasets. The results are divided into four sections, viz. (I) the 'ideal' baseline results achieved by the LSTM-RNN classifier on the manual transcription and acoustic views, (II) the 'practical' baseline results achieved with the imperfect ASR view, (III) the results obtained, for the practical scenario, by the proposed approach with DCCA enhanced views and (IV) the improvement on using DCCA enhanced acoustic view with manual transcriptions.

Table 1: Sentiment classification performance using a bi-directional LSTM-RNN classifier.

		MOSI		MOSEI	
		Acc.	F1	Acc.	F1
	AU	50.6	50.0	59.4	58.0
I	MT	73.5	73.1	68.7	68.6
	MT+AU	71.4	71.0	68.7	68.7
II	AT	69.1	68.6	68.0	67.5
	AT+AU	69.4	69.2	68.1	67.9
	$AU_\uparrow$	51.6	51.1	58.9	59.3
III	$AT_\uparrow$	70.2	69.7	68.8	68.7
	$AT_\uparrow+AU_\uparrow$	**70.9**	**70.7**	**69.1**	**69.0**
IV	$MT+AU_\uparrow$	**74.6**	**74.1**	**69.4**	**69.3**

5 Discussion

5.1 Performance of ASR view (AT)

Comparison of MT and AT views in sections I and II of Table 1 shows that the AT view degrades the classification performance Accuracy and F-score reduce by 4.4% and 4.5% absolute for CMU-MOSI and by 0.6% and 0.8% absolute for CMU-MOSEI[1]. Similarly, degradations are also present in the bimodal setup (MT+AU vs AT+AU).

5.2 Performance of acoustic view (AU)

The acoustic view (AU) in itself gives a poor performance for CMU-MOSI and a relatively better performance for CMU-MOSEI. However, when fused along with the language views (MT or AT), it results in small or no improvement and sometimes a degradation. This indicates that the raw acoustic views or its existing representations may not always contribute for sentiment classification, due to the existence of encoded and decoded sentiments as discussed in (Chakraborty et al., 2018).

5.3 Improvements with DCCA

As discussed above, the ASR and acoustic views (AT and AU) reduced the classification scores. Section III of Table 1 shows that our approach to enhance the imperfect views using DCCA can lead to significant improvements. ASR view (AT vs $AT_\uparrow$) F-scores improve by 1.1% (CMU-MOSI) and 1.2% (CMU-MOSEI) absolute. Acoustic view (AU vs $AU_\uparrow$) F-scores improve by 1.1% (CMU-MOSI) and 1.3% (CMU-MOSEI) absolute. F-scores for the bimodal system with ASR view (AT+AU vs $AT_\uparrow+AU_\uparrow$) improve by 1.5% (CMU-MOSI) and 1.1% (CMU-MOSEI) absolute. Bimodal system with manual transcription and DCCA enhanced acoustic view (MT+AU vs $MT+AU_\uparrow$) also shows F-score improvements, of 3.1% (CMU-MOSI) and 0.6% (CMU-MOSEI).

5.4 ASR view improvements with non contextual classifier

As discussed in (Poria et al., 2017), the bi-directional LSTM-RNN exploits contextual information from the adjacent utterances and the entire video. In order to obtain the improvements due to DCCA alone we evaluated the performances of MT, AT and $AT_\uparrow$ with a non contextual classifier. We trained logistic regression models which classify the utterance level CNN representations independently into positive and negative sentiments. Table 2 reports the resulting % accuracies. ASR view (AT vs $AT_\uparrow$) accuracies improve by 1.4% and 1.9% absolute due to DCCA.

Table 2: Improvement in ASR view accuracy using a non contextual classifier.

	MOSI	MOSEI
MT	71.1	67.5
AT	63.7	63.8
$AT_\uparrow$	65.1	65.7

6 Conclusion

Erroneous ASR views and weak acoustic views of videos can degrade sentiment classification performance in practical scenarios. We observed degradations (up to 4.5% absolute) in F-score on standard CMU-MOSI dataset, using a popular ASR setup and an utterance level contextual LSTM-RNN classifier The effect could be more severe on multimodal systems relying on word level fusion. Our approach to improve the imperfect views using canonical correlation analysis shows significant improvements (up to 3.1% absolute).

---

[1] We found that manual transcriptions of several utterances in the CMU-MOSEI dataset are unreliable and hence its performance of MT would be higher than that obtained.

References

Galen Andrew, Raman Arora, Jeff Bilmes, and Karen Livescu. 2013. Deep canonical correlation analysis. In *Proceedings of the International Conference on Machine Learning*, volume 28, pages 1247–1255.

T. Athanaselis, S. Bakamidis, I. Dologlou, R. Cowie, E. Douglas-Cowie, and C. Cox. 2005. Asr for emotional speech: Clarifying the issues and enhancing performance. *Neural Netw.*, 18(4):437–444.

Rupayan Chakraborty, Meghna Pandharipande, and Sunil Kumar Kopparapu. 2018. *Analyzing Emotion in Spontaneous Speech*, 1st edition. Springer Publishing Company, Incorporated.

Minghai Chen, Sen Wang, Paul Pu Liang, Tadas Baltrusaitis, Amir Zadeh, and Louis-Philippe Morency. 2018. Multimodal sentiment analysis with word-level fusion and reinforcement learning. *CoRR*, abs/1802.00924.

Florian Eyben, Felix Weninger, Martin Woellmer, and Bjoern Schuller. 2009. openSMILE. http://www.audeering.com/research/opensmile. Accessed: 2017.

Yifan Gong. 1995. Speech recognition in noisy environments: A survey. *Speech Commun.*, 16(3):261–291.

A. Graves and J. Schmidhuber. 2005. Framewise phoneme classification with bidirectional lstm networks. In *Proceedings of International Joint Conference on Neural Networks*, pages 2047–2052.

Alex Graves, Marcus Liwicki, Horst Bunke, Jürgen Schmidhuber, and Santiago Fernández. 2008. Unconstrained on-line handwriting recognition with recurrent neural networks. In *Advances in Neural Information Processing Systems 20*, pages 577–584.

Yoon Kim. 2014. Convolutional neural networks for sentence classification. In *EMNLP*, pages 1746–1751.

J. Li, L. Deng, Y. Gong, and R. Haeb-Umbach. 2014. An overview of noise-robust automatic speech recognition. *IEEE Transactions on Audio, Speech, and Language Processing*, 22(4):745–777.

Behnaz Nojavanasghari, Deepak Gopinath, Jayanth Koushik, Tadas Baltrušaitis, and Louis-Philippe Morency. 2016. Deep multimodal fusion for persuasiveness prediction. In *ICMI*, pages 284–288.

V. Peddinti, G. Chen, V. Manohar, T. Ko, D. Povey, and S. Khudanpur. 2015. Jhu aspire system: Robust lvcsr with tdnns, ivector adaptation and rnn-lms. In *2015 IEEE Workshop on Automatic Speech Recognition and Understanding (ASRU)*, pages 539–546.

Jeffrey Pennington, Richard Socher, and Christopher D Manning. 2014. Glove: Global vectors for word representation. In *EMNLP*, pages 1532–1543.

Verónica Pérez-Rosas, Rada Mihalcea, and Louis Philippe Morency. 2013. Utterance-level multimodal sentiment analysis. In *Proceedings of the 51st Annual Meeting of the Association for Computational Linguistics*, pages 973–982.

Soujanya Poria, Erik Cambria, Devamanyu Hazarika, Navonil Majumder, Amir Zadeh, and Louis-Philippe Morency. 2017. Context-dependent sentiment analysis in user-generated videos. In *Proceedings of the 55th Annual Meeting of the Association for Computational Linguistics*, pages 873–883.

Daniel Povey. 2017. Kaldi models. http://kaldi-asr.org/models.html.

Daniel Povey et. al. 2011. The kaldi speech recognition toolkit. In *IEEE Workshop on Automatic Speech Recognition and Understanding*.

Shyam Sundar Rajagopalan, Louis-Philippe Morency, Tadas Baltrusaitis, and Roland Goecke. 2016. Extending long short-term memory for multi-view structured learning. In *Computer Vision – ECCV 2016*, pages 338–353.

J. Shao, Z. Zhao, F. Su, and T. Yue. 2015. 3view deep canonical correlation analysis for cross-modal retrieval. In *2015 Visual Communications and Image Processing (VCIP)*, pages 1–4.

I. Sheikh, D. Fohr, and I. Illina. 2017. Topic segmentation in asr transcripts using bidirectional rnns for change detection. In *IEEE Workshop on Automatic Speech Recognition and Understanding*, pages 512–518.

W. Wang, R. Arora, K. Livescu, and J. A. Bilmes. 2015. Unsupervised learning of acoustic features via deep canonical correlation analysis. In *ICASSP*, pages 4590–4594.

Chang Xu, Dacheng Tao, and Chao Xu. 2013. A survey on multi-view learning. *CoRR*, abs/1304.5634.

Amir Zadeh. 2018a. CMU-MOSEI dataset. http://multicomp.cs.cmu.edu/resources/cmu-mosei-dataset/. Accessed: 2018.

Amir Zadeh. 2018b. CMU Multimodal Data SDK. https://github.com/A2Zadeh/CMU-MultimodalDataSDK. Accessed: 2018.

Amir Zadeh, Minghai Chen, Soujanya Poria, Erik Cambria, and Louis-Philippe Morency. 2017. Tensor fusion network for multimodal sentiment analysis. *CoRR*, abs/1707.07250.

Amir Zadeh, Paul Pu Liang, Navonil Mazumder, Soujanya Poria, Erik Cambria, and Louis-Philippe Morency. 2018. Memory fusion network for multi-view sequential learning. *CoRR*, abs/1802.00927.

Amir Zadeh, Rowan Zellers, Eli Pincus, and Louis-Philippe Morency. 2016. MOSI: multimodal corpus of sentiment intensity and subjectivity analysis in online opinion videos. *CoRR*, abs/1606.06259.

Polarity and Intensity: the Two Aspects of Sentiment Analysis

Leimin Tian
School of Informatics
the University of Edinburgh
Leimin.Tian@monash.edu

Catherine Lai
School of Informatics
the University of Edinburgh
clai@inf.ed.ac.uk

Johanna D. Moore
School of Informatics
the University of Edinburgh
J.Moore@ed.ac.uk

Abstract

Current multimodal sentiment analysis frames sentiment score prediction as a general Machine Learning task. However, what the sentiment score actually represents has often been overlooked. As a measurement of opinions and affective states, a sentiment score generally consists of two aspects: polarity and intensity. We decompose sentiment scores into these two aspects and study how they are conveyed through individual modalities and combined multimodal models in a naturalistic monologue setting. In particular, we build unimodal and multimodal multi-task learning models with sentiment score prediction as the main task and polarity and/or intensity classification as the auxiliary tasks. Our experiments show that sentiment analysis benefits from multi-task learning, and individual modalities differ when conveying the polarity and intensity aspects of sentiment.

1 Introduction

Computational analysis of human multimodal language is a growing research area in Natural Language Processing (NLP). One important type of information communicated through human multimodal language is sentiment. Current NLP studies often define sentiments using scores on a scale, e.g., a 5-point Likert scale representing sentiments from strongly negative to strongly positive. Previous work on multimodal sentiment analysis has focused on identifying effective approaches for sentiment score prediction (e.g., Zadeh et al. (2018b)). However, in these studies sentiment score prediction is typically represented as a regression or classification task, without taking into account what the sentiment score means. As a measurement of human opinions and affective states, a sentiment score can often be decomposed into two aspects: the polarity and intensity of the sentiment. In this work, we study how individual modalities and multimodal information convey these two aspects of sentiment.

More specifically, we conduct experiments on the Carnegie Mellon University Multimodal Opinion Sentiment Intensity (CMU-MOSI) database (Zadeh et al., 2016). The CMU-MOSI database is a widely used benchmark database for multimodal sentiment analysis. It contains naturalistic monologues expressing opinions on various subjects. Sentiments are annotated as continuous scores for each opinion segment in the CMU-MOSI database, and data were collected over the vocal, visual, and verbal modalities. We build unimodal and multimodal multi-task learning models with sentiment score regression as the main task, and polarity and/or intensity classification as the auxiliary tasks. Our main research questions are:

1. Does sentiment score prediction benefit from multi-task learning?
2. Do individual modalities convey the polarity and intensity of sentiment differently?
3. Does multi-task learning influence unimodal and multimodal sentiment analysis models in different ways?

Our work contributes to our current understanding of the intra-modal and inter-modal dynamics of how sentiments are communicated in human multimodal language. Moreover, our study provides detailed analysis on how multi-task learning and modality fusion influences sentiment analysis.

2 Background

Sentiment is an important type of information conveyed in human language. Previous sentiment

Proceedings of the First Grand Challenge and Workshop on Human Multimodal Language (Challenge-HML), pages 40–47,
Melbourne, Australia July 20, 2018. ©2018 Association for Computational Linguistics

analysis studies in the field of NLP have mostly been focused on the verbal modality (i.e., text). For example, predicting the sentiment of Twitter texts (Kouloumpis et al., 2011) or news articles (Balahur et al., 2013). However, human language is multimodal in, for instance, face-to-face communication and online multimedia opinion sharing. Understanding natural language used in such scenarios is especially important for NLP applications in Human-Computer/Robot Interaction. Thus, in recent years there has been growing interest in multimodal sentiment analysis. The three most widely studied modalities in current multimodal sentiment analysis research are: vocal (e.g., speech acoustics), visual (e.g., facial expressions), and verbal (e.g., lexical content). These are sometimes referred to as "the three Vs" of communication (Mehrabian et al., 1971). Multimodal sentiment analysis research focuses on understanding how an individual modality conveys sentiment information (intra-modal dynamics), and how they interact with each other (inter-modal dynamics). It is a challenging research area and state-of-the-art performance of automatic sentiment prediction has room for improvement compared to human performance (Zadeh et al., 2018a).

While multimodal approaches to sentiment analysis are relatively new in NLP, multimodal emotion recognition has long been a focus of Affective Computing. For example, De Silva and Ng (2000) combined facial expressions and speech acoustics to predict the Big-6 emotion categories (Ekman, 1992). Emotions and sentiments are closely related concepts in Psychology and Cognitive Science research, and are often used interchangeably. Munezero et al. (2014) identified the main differences between sentiments and emotions to be that sentiments are more stable and dispositional than emotions, and sentiments are formed and directed toward a specific object. However, when adopting the cognitive definition of emotions which connects emotions to stimuli in the environment (Ortony et al., 1990), the boundary between emotions and sentiments blurs. In particular, the circumplex model of emotions proposed by Russell (1980) describes emotions with two dimensions: Arousal which represents the level of excitement (active/inactive), and Valence which represents the level of liking (positive/negative). In many sentiment analysis studies, sentiments are defined using Likert

scales with varying numbers of steps. For example, the Stanford Sentiment Treebank (Socher et al., 2013) used a 7-point Likert scale to annotate sentiments. Such sentiment annotation schemes have two aspects: polarity (positive/negative values) and intensity (steps within the positive or negative range of values). This similarity suggests connections between emotions defined in terms of Valence and Arousal, and sentiments defined with polarity and intensity, as shown in Table 1. However, while previous work on multimodal emotion recognition often predicts Arousal and Valence separately, most previous work on multimodal sentiment analysis generally predicts the sentiment score as a single number. Thus, we are motivated to study how the polarity and intensity aspects of sentiments are each conveyed.

Aspect of the affect	Activeness	Liking
Emotion as by Russell (1980)	Arousal	Valence
Sentiment on a Likert scale	Intensity	Polarity

Table 1: Similarity between circumplex model of emotion and Likert scale based sentiment.

In order to decompose sentiment scores into polarity and intensity and study how they are conveyed through different modalities, we include polarity and/or intensity classification as auxiliary tasks to sentiment score prediction with multi-task learning. One problem with Machine Learning approaches for Affective Computing is model robustness. In multi-task learning, the model shares representations between the main task and auxiliary tasks related to the main task, often enabling the model to generalize better on the main task (Ruder, 2017). Multiple auxiliary tasks have been used in previous sentiment analysis and emotion recognition studies. For example, Xia and Liu (2017) used dimensional emotion regression as an auxiliary task for categorical emotion classification, while Chen et al. (2017) used sentence type classification (number of opinion targets expressed in a sentence) as an auxiliary task for verbal sentiment analysis. To the best of our knowledge, there has been no previous work applying multi-task learning to the CMU-MOSI database.

In addition to how individual modalities convey sentiment, another interesting topic in multimodal sentiment analysis is how to combine information from multiple modalities. There are three main types of modality fusion strategies in current multimodal Machine Learning research (Baltrušaitis et al., 2018): early fusion which combines features from different modalities, late fusion which combines outputs of unimodal models, and hybrid fusion which exploits the advantages of both early and late fusion. We will study the performance of these different modality fusion strategies for multimodal sentiment analysis.

3 Methodology

3.1 The CMU-MOSI Database

The CMU-MOSI database contains 93 YouTube opinion videos from 89 distinct speakers (Zadeh et al., 2016). The videos are monologues on various topics recorded with various setups, lasting from 2 to 5 minutes. 2199 opinion segments were manually identified from the videos with an average length of 4.2 seconds (approximately 154 minutes in total). An opinion segment is the expression of opinion on a distinct subject, and can be part of a spoken utterance or consist of several consecutive utterances. Zadeh et al. (2016) collected sentiment score annotations of the opinion segments using Amazon Mechanical Turk and each video clip was annotated by five workers. For each opinion segment the sentiment scores are annotated on a 7-point Likert scale, i.e., strongly negative (−3), negative (−2), weakly negative (−1), neutral (0), weakly positive (+1), positive (+2), strongly positive (+3). The gold-standard sentiment score annotations provided are the average of all five workers.

Previous work on the CMU-MOSI database explored various approaches to improving performance of sentiment score prediction (e.g., Zadeh et al. (2018b)). The target sentiment annotations can be continuous sentiment scores or discrete sentiment classes (binary, 5-class, or 7-class sentiment classes). The Tensor Fusion Network model of Zadeh et al. (2017) achieved the best performance for continuous sentiment score regression on the CMU-MOSI database using features from all three modalities. The Pearson's correlation coefficient between the automatic predictions of their model and the gold-standard sentiment score annotations reached 0.70. In this work, we follow the parameter settings and features used by Zadeh et al. (2017) when predicting the sentiment scores.

3.2 Multimodal Sentiment Analysis with Multi-Task Learning

In this study, we apply multi-task learning to sentiment analysis using the CMU-MOSI database. We consider predicting the gold-standard sentiment scores as the main task. Thus, the single-task learning model is a regression model predicting the sentiment score S_o of an opinion segment o, which has a value within range $[-3,+3]$. To perform multi-task learning, for each opinion segment, we transform the gold-standard sentiment score S_o into binary polarity class P_o and intensity class I_o:

$$P_o = \begin{cases} \text{Positive}, & \text{if } S_o \geq 0 \\ \text{Negative}, & \text{if } S_o < 0 \end{cases} \quad (1)$$

$$I_o = \begin{cases} \text{Strong}, & \text{if } |S_o| \geq 2.5 \\ \text{Medium}, & \text{if } 1.5 \leq |S_o| < 2.5 \\ \text{Weak}, & \text{if } 0.5 \leq |S_o| < 1.5 \\ \text{Neutral}, & \text{if } |S_o| < 0.5 \end{cases} \quad (2)$$

Unlike previous studies performing a 5-class or 7-class classification experiment for sentiment analysis, our definition of intensity classes uses the absolute sentiment scores, thus separating the polarity and intensity information. For example, an opinion segment o_1 with S_{o_1} = +3.0 will have P_{o_1} = *Positive* and I_{o_1} = *Strong*, while an opinion segment o_2 with S_{o_2} = −2.75 will have P_{o_2} = *Negative* and I_{o_2} = *Strong*. Note that here we group the sentiment scores into discrete intensity classes. In the future we plan to study the gain of preserving the ordinal information between the intensity classes.

For each modality or fusion strategy we build four models: single-task sentiment regression model, bi-task sentiment regression model with polarity classification as the auxiliary task, bi-task sentiment regression model with intensity classification as the auxiliary task, and tri-task sentiment regression model with both polarity and intensity classification as the auxiliary tasks. In the bi-task and tri-task models, the main task loss is assigned a weight of 1.0, while the auxiliary task losses are assigned a weight of 0.5. Structures of the single-task and multi-task learning models only differ at the output layer: for sentiment score regression the output is a single node with tanh activation; for polarity classification the output is a single node with sigmoid activation; for intensity classification the output is 4 nodes with softmax activation. The main task uses mean absolute error as the loss function, while polarity classification uses binary cross-entropy as the loss function, and intensity classification uses categorical cross-entropy as the loss function. Following state-of-the-art on the CMU-MOSI database (Zadeh et al., 2017), during training we used Adam as the optimization function with a learning rate of 0.0005. We use the CMU Multimodal Data Software Development Kit (SDK) (Zadeh et al., 2018a) to load and pre-process the CMU-MOSI database, which splits the 2199 opinion segments into training (1283 segments), validation (229 segments), and test (686 segments) sets.[1] We implement the sentiment analysis models using the Keras deep learning library (Chollet et al., 2015).

3.3 Multimodal Features

For the vocal modality, we use the COVAREP feature set provided by the SDK. These are 74 vocal features including 12 Mel-frequency cepstral coefficients, pitch tracking and voiced/unvoiced segmenting features, glottal source parameters, peak slope parameters, and maxima dispersion quotients. The vocal features are extracted from the audio recordings at a sampling rate of 100Hz. For the visual modality, we use the FACET feature set provided by the SDK. These are 46 visual features including facial indicators of 9 types of emotion (anger, contempt, disgust, fear, joy, sadness, surprise, frustration, and confusion) and movements of 20 facial action units. The visual features are extracted from the speaker's facial region in the video recordings at a sampling rate of 30Hz. Following Zadeh et al. (2017), for the vocal and visual unimodal models, we apply a drop-out rate of 0.2 to the features and build a neural network with three hidden layers of 32 ReLU activation units, as shown in Figure 1.

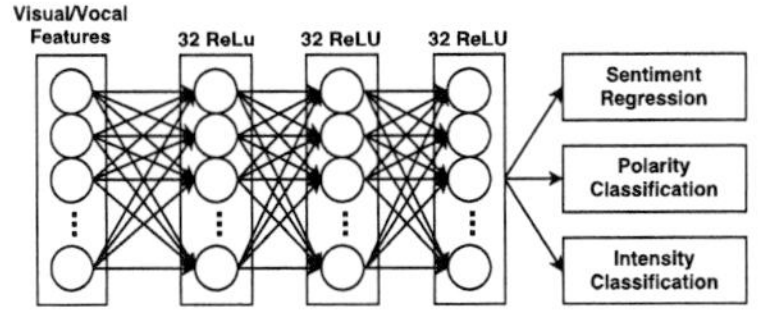

Figure 1: Visual/vocal unimodal tri-task model

For the verbal modality, we use the word em-

bedding features provided by the SDK, which are 300-dimensional GloVe word vectors. There are 26,295 words in total (3,107 unique words) in the opinion segments of the CMU-MOSI database. Following Zadeh et al. (2017), for the verbal unimodal model we build a neural network with one layer of 128 Long Short-Term Memory (LSTM) units and one layer of 64 ReLU activation units, as shown in Figure 2. Previous work has found that context information is important for multimodal sentiment analysis, and the use of LSTM allows us to include history (Poria et al., 2017).

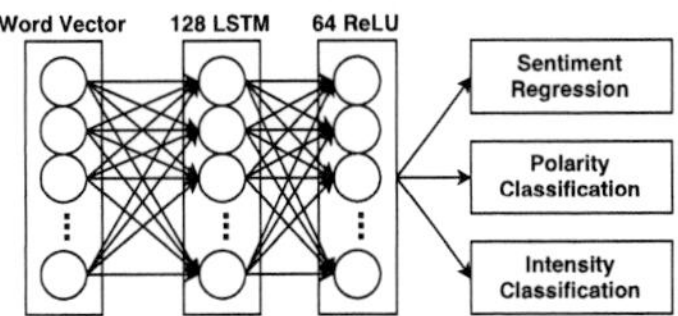

Figure 2: Verbal unimodal tri-task model

Note that the visual and vocal features are extracted at the frame level, while the verbal features are extracted at the word level. Before conducting all unimodal and multimodal experiments, we aligned all the features to the word level using the SDK. This down-samples the visual and vocal features to the word level by computing the averaged feature vectors for all frames within a word.

3.4 Modality Fusion Strategies

We test four fusion strategies here: Early Fusion (EF), Tensor Fusion Network (TFN), Late Fusion (LF), and Hierarchical Fusion (HF). EF and LF are the most widely used fusion strategies in multimodal recognition studies and were shown to be effective for multimodal sentiment analysis (Poria et al., 2015). TFN achieved state-of-the-art performance on the CMU-MOSI database (Zadeh et al., 2017). HF is a form of hybrid fusion strategy shown to be effective for multimodal emotion recognition (Tian et al., 2016).

The structure of the EF model is shown in Figure 3. The feature vectors are simply concatenated in the EF model. A drop-out rate of 0.2 is applied to the combined feature vector. We then stack one layer of 128 LSTM units and three layers of 32 ReLU units with an L2 regularizer weight of 0.01 on top of the multimodal inputs. To compare performance of the fusion strategies, this same structure is applied to the multimodal inputs in all multimodal models. In the TFN model, we compute

---

[1] Segment 13 of video 8qrpnFRGt2A is partially missing and thus removed for the experiments.

the Cartesian products (shown in Figure 4) of the unimodal model top layers as the multimodal inputs. Unlike Zadeh et al. (2017), we did not add the extra constant dimension with value 1 when computing the 3-fold Cartesian space in order to reduce the dimensionality of the multimodal input. In the LF model, as shown in Figure 5, we concatenate the unimodal model top layers as the multimodal inputs. In the HF model, unimodal information is used in a hierarchy where the top layer of the lower unimodal model is concatenated with the input layer of the higher unimodal model, as shown in Figure 6. We use the vocal modality at the bottom of the hierarchy while using the verbal modality at the top in HF fusion. This is because in previous studies (e.g., Zadeh et al. (2018a)) the verbal modality was shown to be the most effective for unimodal sentiment analysis, while the vocal modality was shown to be the least effective.

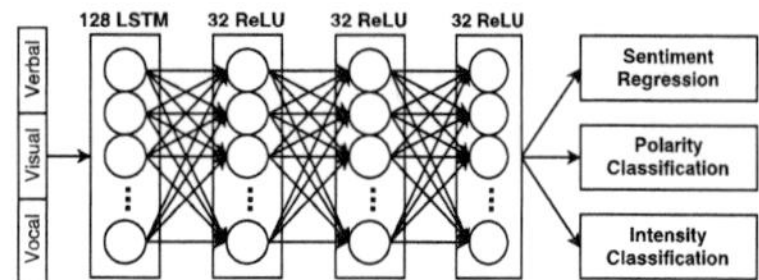

Figure 3: Structure of EF tri-task model

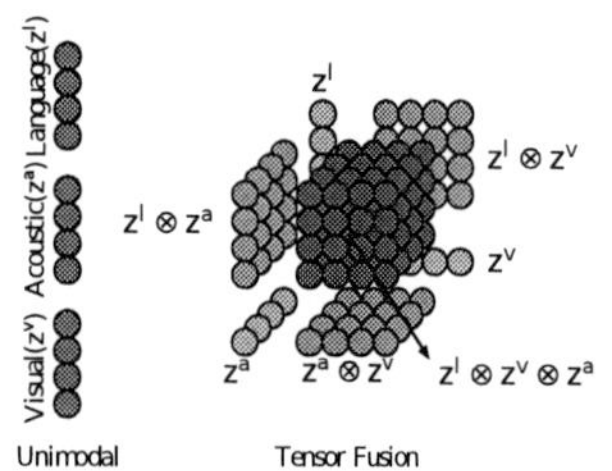

Figure 4: Fusion strategy of the TFN model (Zadeh et al., 2017)

4 Experiments and Results

Here we report our sentiment score prediction experiments.[2] In Tables 2 and 3, "S" is the single-task learning model; "S+P" is the bi-task learning model with polarity classification as the auxillary task; "S+I" is the bi-task learning model with intensity classification as the auxillary task; "S+P+I" is the tri-task learning model. To evaluate the performance of sentiment score prediction, following previous work (Zadeh et al., 2018a), we

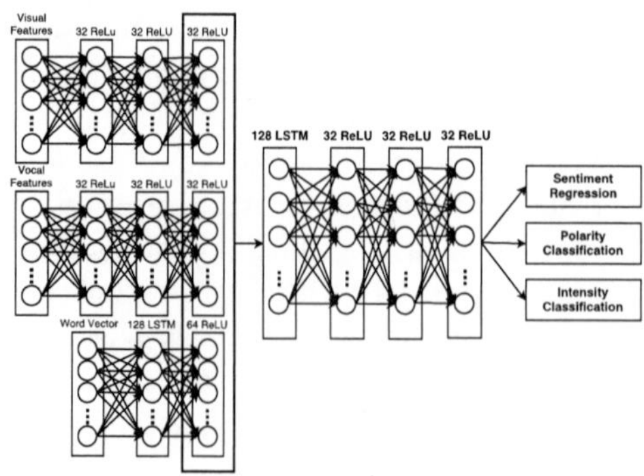

Figure 5: Structure of LF tri-task model

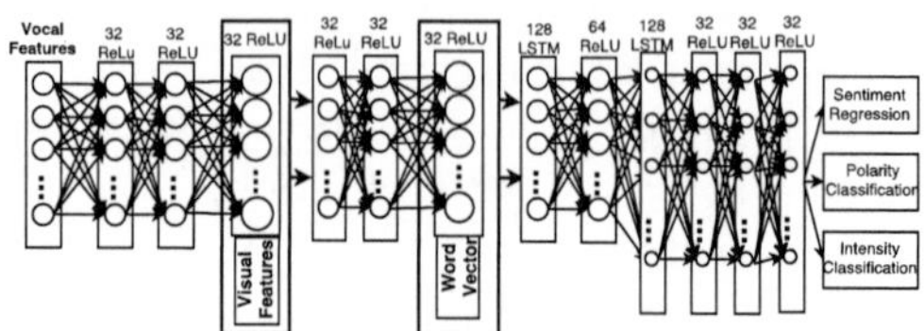

Figure 6: Structure of HF tri-task model

report both Pearson's correlation coefficient (CC, higher is better) and mean absolute error (MAE, lower is better) between predictions and annotations of sentiment scores on the test set. In each row of Tables 2 and 3, the numbers in bold are the best performance for each modality or fusion strategy. To identify the significant differences in results, we perform a two-sample Wilcoxon test on the sentiment score predictions given by each pair of models being compared and consider $p < 0.05$ as significant. We also include random prediction as a baseline and the human performance reported by Zadeh et al. (2017).

4.1 Unimodal Experiments

The results of unimodal sentiment prediction experiments are shown in Table 2.[3] The verbal models have the best performance here, which is consistent with previous sentiment analysis studies on multiple databases (e.g., Zadeh et al. (2018a)). This suggests that lexical information remains the most effective for sentiment analysis. On each modality, the best performance is achieved by a multi-task learning model. This answers our first research question and suggests that sentiment analysis can benefit from multi-task learning.

[2]Source code available at: https://github.com/tianleimin/.

[3]All unimodal models have significantly different performance. $p = 0.009$ for S+P and S+P+I Visual models, $p \ll 0.001$ for Visual and Vocal S+I models.

In multi-task learning, the main task gains additional information from the auxillary tasks. Compared to the S model, the S+P model has increased focus on the polarity of sentiment, while the S+I model has increased focus on the intensity of sentiment. On the verbal modality, the S+P model achieved the best performance, while on the visual modality the S+I model achieved the best performance. This suggests that the verbal modality is weaker at communicating the polarity of sentiment. Thus, verbal sentiment analysis benefits more from including additional information on polarity. On the contrary, the visual modality is weaker at communicating the intensity of sentiment. Thus, visual sentiment analysis benefits more from including additional information on intensity. For the vocal modality, the S+P+I model achieved the best performance, and the S+P model yielded improved performance over that of the S model. This suggests that the vocal modality is weaker at communicating the polarity of sentiment. Thus, addressing our second research question, the results suggest that individual modalities differ when conveying each aspect of sentiment.

CC	S	S+P	S+I	S+P+I
Random	–	–	–	–
Vocal	0.125	0.149	0.119	**0.153**
Visual	0.092	0.109	**0.116**	0.106
Verbal	0.404	**0.455**	0.434	0.417
Human	0.820	–	–	–
MAE	**S**	**S+P**	**S+I**	**S+P+I**
Random	1.880	–	–	–
Vocal	1.456	1.471	1.444	**1.431**
Visual	1.442	**1.439**	1.453	1.460
Verbal	1.196	**1.156**	1.181	1.206
Human	0.710	–	–	–

Table 2: Unimodal sentiment analysis results on the CMU-MOSI test set. Numbers in bold are the best results on each modality.

4.2 Multimodal Experiments

The results of the multimodal experiments are shown in Table 3. We find that EF>HF>TFN>LF.[4] The reason that the EF model yields the best performance may be that it is the least complex. This is shown to be beneficial for the small CMU-MOSI database (Poria et al., 2015). Unlike Zadeh et al. (2017), here the EF model outperforms the TFN model. However, the TFN model achieved the best performance on the training and validation sets. This indicates that performance of the TFN model may be limited by over-fitting. Compared to the feature concatenation used in EF, the Cartesian product used in TFN results in higher dimensionality of the multimodal input vector,[5] which in turn increases the complexity of the model. Similarly, the HF model has worse performance than the EF model here, unlike in Tian et al. (2016). This may be due to the HF model having the deepest structure with the most hidden layers, which increases its complexity.

The performance of unimodal and multimodal models are significantly different. In general, the multimodal models have better performance than the unimodal models.[6] Unlike unimodal models, multimodal models benefit less from multi-task learning. In fact, the HF and LF models have better performance using single-task learning. For the TFN models, only the S+P model outperforms the S model, although the improvement is not significant.[7] For the EF models, multi-task learning results in better performance.[8] The reason that EF benefits from multi-task learning may be that it combines modalities without bias and individual features have more influence on the EF model. Thus, the benefit of multi-task learning is preserved in EF. However, the other fusion strategies (TFN, LF, HF) attempt to compensate one modality with information from other modalities, i.e., relying more on other modalities when one modality is weaker at predicting an aspect of sentiment. In Section 4.1 we showed that each modality has different weaknesses when conveying the polarity or intensity aspect of sentiment. The multimodal models are able to overcome such weaknesses by modality fusion. Thus, multi-task learning does not yield additional improvement in these models. Our observations answer our third research question: multi-task learning influences unimodal and

---

[4]Performance of multimodal models are significantly different, except that the HF S and the TFN S+P model have $p = 0.287$. $p = 0.001$ for EF S+P+I and HF S, $p = 0.017$ for TFN S+P and LF S.

[5]Dimension of the EF input is 420, for TFN is 65,536.

[6]Except that the LF models often have worse performance than the verbal S+P model. $p << 0.001$ for TFN S+P and verbal S+P, $p = 0.017$ for verbal S+P and LF S.

[7]$p = 0.105$ for S TFN and S+P TFN.

[8]$p = 0.888$ for S EF and S+P EF, $p = 0.029$ for S EF and S+I EF, $p = 0.009$ for S EF and S+P+I EF.

multimodal sentiment analysis differently.

CC	S	S+P	S+I	S+P+I
Random	–	–	–	–
EF	0.471	0.472	0.476	**0.482**
TFN	0.448	**0.461**	0.446	0.429
LF	**0.454**	0.413	0.428	0.428
HF	**0.469**	0.424	0.458	0.432
Human	0.820	–	–	–
MAE	**S**	**S+P**	**S+I**	**S+P+I**
Random	1.880	–	–	–
EF	1.197	1.181	1.193	**1.172**
TFN	1.186	1.181	**1.178**	1.205
LF	**1.179**	1.211	1.204	1.201
HF	**1.155**	1.211	1.164	1.187
Human	0.710	–	–	–

Table 3: Multimodal sentiment analysis results on the CMU-MOSI test set. Numbers in bold are the best results for each fusion strategy in each row.

5 Discussion

Our unimodal experiments in Section 4.1 show that unimodal sentiment analysis benefits significantly from multi-task learning. As suggested by Wilson (2008), polarity and intensity can be conveyed through different units of language. We can use one word such as *extremely* to express intensity, while the polarity of a word and the polarity of the opinion segment the word is in may be opposite. Our work supports a fine-grained sentiment analysis. By including polarity and intensity classification as the auxiliary tasks, we illustrate that individual modalities differ when conveying sentiment. In particular, the visual modality is weaker at conveying the intensity aspect of sentiment, while the vocal and verbal modalities are weaker at conveying the polarity aspect of sentiment. In previous emotion recognition studies under the circumplex model of emotions (Russell, 1980), it was found that the visual modality is typically weaker at conveying the Arousal dimension of emotion, while the vocal modality is typically weaker at conveying the Valence dimension of emotion (e.g., Nicolaou et al. (2011)). The similarities between the performance of different communication modalities on conveying emotion dimensions and on conveying different aspects of sentiment indicate a connection between emotion dimensions and sentiment. The different behav-

iors of unimodal models in conveying the polarity and intensity aspects of sentiment also explain the improved performance achieved by modality fusion in Section 4.2 and in various previous studies. By decomposing sentiment scores into polarity and intensity, our work provides detailed understanding on how individual modalities and multimodal information convey these two aspects of sentiment.

We are aware that performance of our sentiment analysis models leaves room for improvement compared to state-of-the-art on the CMU-MOSI database. One reason may be that we did not perform pre-training in this study. In the future, we plan to explore more advanced learning techniques and models, such as a Dynamic Fusion Graph (Zadeh et al., 2018b), to improve performance. We also plan to perform case studies to provide detailed analysis on how the unimodal models benefit from multi-task learning, and how individual modalities compensate each other in the multimodal models.

6 Conclusions

In this work, we decouple Likert scale sentiment scores into two aspects: polarity and intensity, and study the influence of including polarity and/or intensity classification as auxiliary tasks to sentiment score regression. Our experiments showed that all unimodal models and some multimodal models benefit from multi-task learning. Our unimodal experiments indicated that each modality conveys different aspects of sentiment differently. In addition, we observed similar behaviors between how individual modalities convey the polarity and intensity aspects of sentiments and how they convey the Valence and Arousal emotion dimensions. Such connections between sentiments and emotions encourage researchers to obtain an integrated view of sentiment analysis and emotion recognition. Our multimodal experiments showed that unlike unimodal models, multimodal models benefit less from multi-task learning. This suggests that one reason that modality fusion yields improved performance in sentiment analysis is its ability to combine the different strengths of individual modalities on conveying sentiments.

Note that we only conducted experiments on the CMU-MOSI database. In the future, we plan to expand our study to multiple databases. Moreover, we are interested in including databases collected on modalities beyond the three Vs. For example, gestures or physiological signals. We also plan to perform sentiment analysis and emotion recognition in a multi-task learning setting to further explore the relationship between sentiments and emotions.

Acknowledgments

We would like to thank Zack Hodari for his support on computational resources, and Jennifer Williams for the insightful discussion.

References

Alexandra Balahur, Ralf Steinberger, Mijail Kabadjov, Vanni Zavarella, Erik Van Der Goot, Matina Halkia, Bruno Pouliquen, and Jenya Belyaeva. 2013. Sentiment analysis in the news. *arXiv preprint arXiv:1309.6202*.

Tadas Baltrušaitis, Chaitanya Ahuja, and Louis-Philippe Morency. 2018. Multimodal machine learning: A survey and taxonomy. *IEEE Transactions on Pattern Analysis and Machine Intelligence*.

Tao Chen, Ruifeng Xu, Yulan He, and Xuan Wang. 2017. Improving sentiment analysis via sentence type classification using BiLSTM-CRF and CNN. *Expert Systems with Applications*, 72:221–230.

François Chollet et al. 2015. Keras. `https://keras.io`.

Liyanage C De Silva and Pei Chi Ng. 2000. Bimodal emotion recognition. In *FG*, pages 332–335. IEEE.

Paul Ekman. 1992. An argument for basic emotions. *Cognition & Emotion*, 6(3-4):169–200.

Efthymios Kouloumpis, Theresa Wilson, and Johanna D Moore. 2011. Twitter sentiment analysis: The good the bad and the omg! *ICWSM*, 11(538-541):164.

Albert Mehrabian et al. 1971. *Silent messages*, volume 8. Wadsworth Belmont, CA.

Myriam D Munezero, Calkin Suero Montero, Erkki Sutinen, and John Pajunen. 2014. Are they different? affect, feeling, emotion, sentiment, and opinion detection in text. *IEEE Transactions on Affective Computing*, 5(2):101–111.

Mihalis A Nicolaou, Hatice Gunes, and Maja Pantic. 2011. Continuous prediction of spontaneous affect from multiple cues and modalities in valence-arousal space. *IEEE Transactions on Affective Computing*, 2(2):92–105.

Andrew Ortony, Gerald L Clore, and Allan Collins. 1990. *The cognitive structure of emotions*. Cambridge University Press.

Soujanya Poria, Erik Cambria, and Alexander Gelbukh. 2015. Deep convolutional neural network textual features and multiple kernel learning for utterance-level multimodal sentiment analysis. In *Proceedings of the 2015 conference on empirical methods in natural language processing*, pages 2539–2544.

Soujanya Poria, Erik Cambria, Devamanyu Hazarika, Navonil Majumder, Amir Zadeh, and Louis-Philippe Morency. 2017. Context-dependent sentiment analysis in user-generated videos. In *Proceedings of the 55th Annual Meeting of the Association for Computational Linguistics (Volume 1: Long Papers)*, volume 1, pages 873–883.

Sebastian Ruder. 2017. An overview of multi-task learning in deep neural networks. *arXiv preprint arXiv:1706.05098*.

James A Russell. 1980. A circumplex model of affect. *Journal of Personality and Social Psychology*, 39(6):1161.

Richard Socher, Alex Perelygin, Jean Wu, Jason Chuang, Christopher D Manning, Andrew Ng, and Christopher Potts. 2013. Recursive deep models for semantic compositionality over a sentiment treebank. In *EMNLP*, pages 1631–1642.

Leimin Tian, Johanna Moore, and Catherine Lai. 2016. Recognizing emotions in spoken dialogue with hierarchically fused acoustic and lexical features. In *SLT*, pages 565–572. IEEE.

Theresa Ann Wilson. 2008. *Fine-grained subjectivity and sentiment analysis: recognizing the intensity, polarity, and attitudes of private states*. University of Pittsburgh.

Rui Xia and Yang Liu. 2017. A multi-task learning framework for emotion recognition using 2d continuous space. *IEEE Transactions on Affective Computing*, 8(1):3–14.

A Zadeh, PP Liang, S Poria, P Vij, E Cambria, and LP Morency. 2018a. Multi-attention recurrent network for human communication comprehension. In *AAAI*.

Amir Zadeh, Minghai Chen, Soujanya Poria, Erik Cambria, and Louis-Philippe Morency. 2017. Tensor fusion network for multimodal sentiment analysis. In *EMNLP*, pages 1103–1114.

Amir Zadeh, Paul Pu Liang, Jon Vanbriesen, Soujanya Poria, Erik Cambria, Minghai Chen, and Louis-Philippe Morency. 2018b. Multimodal language analysis in the wild: CMU-MOSEI dataset and interpretable dynamic fusion graph. In *Association for Computational Linguistics (ACL)*.

Amir Zadeh, Rowan Zellers, Eli Pincus, and Louis-Philippe Morency. 2016. Multimodal sentiment intensity analysis in videos: Facial gestures and verbal messages. *IEEE Intelligent Systems*, 31(6):82–88.

ASR-based Features for Emotion Recognition: A Transfer Learning Approach

Noé Tits, Kevin El Haddad, Thierry Dutoit
Numediart Institute,
University of Mons, Belgium
{noe.tits, kevin.elhaddad, thierry.dutoit}@umons.ac.be

Abstract

During the last decade, the applications of signal processing have drastically improved with deep learning. However areas of affecting computing such as emotional speech synthesis or emotion recognition from spoken language remains challenging. In this paper, we investigate the use of a neural Automatic Speech Recognition (ASR) as a feature extractor for emotion recognition. We show that these features outperform the eGeMAPS feature set to predict the valence and arousal emotional dimensions, which means that the audio-to-text mapping learned by the ASR system contains information related to the emotional dimensions in spontaneous speech. We also examine the relationship between first layers (closer to speech) and last layers (closer to text) of the ASR and valence/arousal.

1 Introduction

With the advent of deep learning, areas of signal processing have been drasctically improved. In the field of speech synthesis, Wavenet (Van Den Oord et al., 2016), a deep neural network for generating raw audio waveforms, outperforms all previous approaches in terms of naturalness. One of the remaining challenges in speech synthesis is to control its emotional dimension (happiness, sadness, amusement, etc.). The work described here is part of a larger project to control as accurately as possible, the emotional state of a sentence being synthesized. For this, we present here exploratory work regarding the analysis of the relationship between the emotional states and the modalities used to express them in speech.

Indeed one of the main problems to develop such a system is the amount of good quality data (naturalistic emotional speech of synthesis quality, i.e. containing no noise of any sorts). This is why we are considering solutions such as synthesis by analysis and transfer learning (Pan and Yang, 2010).

Arousal and valence (Russell, 1980) are among the most, if not the most used dimensions for quantizing emotions. Valence represents the positivity of the emotion whereas arousal represents its activation. Since they represent emotional states, these dimensions are linked to several modalities that we use to express emotions (audio, text, facial expressions, etc.).

It has recently been shown that for emotion recognition, deep learning based systems learn features that outperform handcrafted features (Trigeorgis et al., 2016) (Martinez et al., 2013) (Kim et al., 2017a,b). The use of context and different modalities has also been studied with deep learning models. Poria et al. (2017) focus on the contextual information among utterances in a video while Zadeh et al. (2017, 2018) develop specific architectures to fuse information coming from different modalities.

In this work, with the goal to study the relationship between valence/arousal, and different modalities, we propose to use the internal representation of a speech-to-text system. An Automatic Speech Recognition (ASR) system or speech-to-text system, learns a mapping between two modalities: an audio speech signal and its corresponding transcription. We hypothesize that such a system must also be learning representations of emotional expressions since these are contained intrinsically in both speech (variation or the pitch, the energy, etc.) and text (semantic of the words).

In fact, we show here that the activations of certain neurons in an ASR system, are useful to esti-

Proceedings of the First Grand Challenge and Workshop on Human Multimodal Language (Challenge-HML), pages 48–52,
Melbourne, Australia July 20, 2018. ©2018 Association for Computational Linguistics

mate the arousal and valence dimensions of an audio speech signal. In other words, transfer learning is leveraged by using features learned for an automatic speech recognition (ASR) task to estimate valence and arousal. The advantage of our method is that it allows combining the use of large datasets of speech with transcriptions with limited datasets annotated in emotional dimensions.

An example of transfer learning is the work of Radford et al. (2017). They trained a multiplicative LTSM (Krause et al., 2016) to predict next character based on the previous ones to design a text generator system. The dataset used to train their model was the Amazon review dataset presented in McAuley et al. (2015). Then, they used the representation learned by the model to predict sentiment also available in the dataset, and achieved state of the art prediction.

In this paper, we show that the activations of a deep learning-based ASR system trained on a large database can be used as features for the estimation of arousal and valence values. The features would therefore be extracted from both the audio and text modalities which the ASR system learned to map.

2 ASR-based Features for Emotion Prediction Via Regression

Our goal is to study the relationship between valence/arousal, and audio/text modalities thanks to an ASR system. The main idea is that the ASR system that models the mapping between audio and text might learn a representation of emotional expression. So, for our analyses, we use an ASR system as a feature extractor which feeds a linear regression algorithm to estimate the arousal/valence values. This section describes the whole system. First we present the ASR system used as a feature extractor. We then briefly present the data used and present first results on the data analysis.

2.1 ASR system

The ASR system used is implemented in (Namju and Kyubyong, 2016) and pre-trained on the VCTK dataset (Veaux et al., 2017) containing 44 hours of speech uttered by 109 native speakers of English.

Its architecture consists of a dilated convolution of blocks. Each block is a gated constitutional unit (GCU) with a skip (residual) connection. In other words a Wavenet-like architecture (Van Den Oord et al., 2016). There are 15 layers and 128 GCUs in each layer: 1920 GCUs in total.

To lighten the computational cost, the audio signal is compressed in 20 Mel-Frequency Cepstral Coefficients (MFCCs) and then fed into the system.

2.2 Dataset Used

IEMOCAP Dataset

The "interactive emotional dyadic motion capture database" (IEMOCAP) dataset (Busso et al., 2008) is used in this paper. It consists of audio-visual recordings of 5 sessions of dialogues between male and female subjects. In total it contains 10 speakers and a total of 12 hours of data. The data is segmented in utterances. Each utterance is transcribed and annotated by category of emotions (Ekman, 1992) and a value for emotional dimensions (Russell, 1980) (valence, arousal and dominance) between 1 and 5 representing the dimension's intensity.

In this work, we only use the audio and text modalities as well as the valence and arousal annotations.

Data Analysis and Neural Features

We investigate the relationship between the activation output of the ASR-based system's GCUs and the valence/arousal values by studying the correlations between them. For every utterance and for each speaker of the IEMOCAP dataset, we compute the mean activation of the GCUs of the ASR. The Pearson correlation coefficient is then calculated between the mean activation outputs and the values of valence/arousal of all utterances of the speaker. In the rest of the paper, we will refer to the mean activation of the GCUs as neural features. As an example, the results concerning the female speaker of session 2 is summarized in a heat map represented in Figure 1

Each row of the heat map corresponds to a layer of GCUs. The color is mapped with the Pearson correlation coefficient value.

One can see that correlations exist for both arousal and valence. This suggests that the ASR-based system learns a certain representation of the emotional dimensions.

2.3 Structure of the system

The system is illustrated in Figure 2. As previously mentioned, the ASR system is used as a fea-

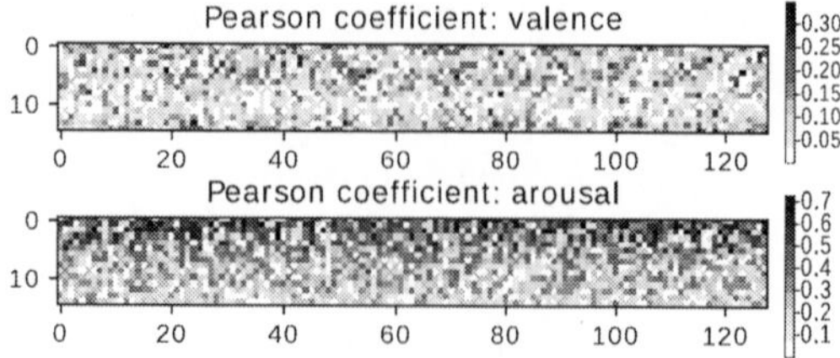

Figure 1: Pearson correlation coefficient between the neural features and valence (up) and arousal (down) - Female speaker of session 2

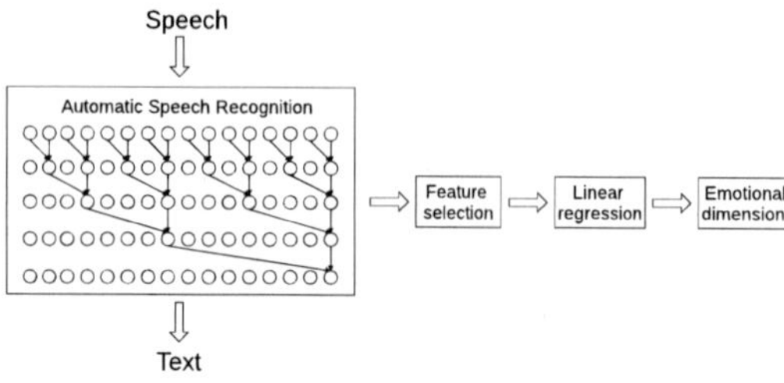

Figure 2: Block diagram of the system

ture extractor. First we compute the 20 MFCCs of the utterances of the IEMOCAP dataset with librosa python library (McFee et al., 2015). These are passed through the ASR to compute the corresponding neural features.

A feature selection is applied on the neural features to keep 100 among the 1920 features for dimensionality reduction purpose. The selection is done using the scikit-learn python library (Pedregosa et al., 2011) with the Fisher score.

Finally a linear regression is trained to estimate the valence/arousal values from the neural features using the IEMOCAP data. The linear regression is done using scikit-learn. The training is done by minimizing the Mean Squared Error (MSE) between predictions and labels.

3   Experiments and Results

In this section, we detail the experiments that we carried out. The first one is the evaluation of the neural features in terms of MSE and its comparison with a linear regression of the eGeMAPS feature set (Eyben et al., 2016). In the second one, we investigate the relationship between the audio and text and modalities and the emotional dimensions.

3.1   First experiment: Linear regression

In this first experiment, we investigate the performance of a linear regression to predict arousal and valence using the neural features. We compare this with a linear regression using the eGeMAPS feature set.

The eGeMAPS feature set is a selection of acoustic features that provide a common baseline for evaluation in researches to avoid differences of feature set and implementations. Indeed, they also provide their implementation with openS-MILE toolkit (Eyben et al., 2010) that we used in this work.

The features were selected based on their ability to represent affective physiological nuances in voice production, their proven performance in former research work as well as the possibility to extract them automatically, and their theoretical significance.

The result of this selection is a set of 18 Low-level descriptors (LLDs) related to frequency (pitch, formants etc.), energy (loudness, Harmonics-to-Noise Ratio, etc.) and spectral balance (spectral slopes, ratios between formant energies, etc.). Then several functionals such as standard deviation and mean are applied to these LLDs to have the final features.

The results obtained from the linear regression in terms of MSE are compared to the annotations for each of the arousal and valence values (between 1 and 5) in Table 1.

	Arousal		Valence	
	Mean	Variance	Mean	Variance
Neural features	**0.259**	0.020	**0.660**	0.118
eGeMAPS set	0.267	0.034	0.697	0.135

Table 1: MSE on the prediction of valence and arousal.

We perform a leave-one-speaker-out evaluation scheme with both feature sets for cross-validation. In other words, each validation set in constituted with the utterances corresponding to one speaker and the corresponding training set with the other speakers. We train a model with each training set and evaluate it on the validation set in terms of MSE. The table contains the mean and standard deviation of the MSEs.

It is clear from this table that the neural features outperform the eGeMAPS in this experiment. This confirms the fact that the ASR system learns representations of emotional dimensions in spontaneous speech.

3.2 Second experiment: Influence of modalities

During the data exploration, we noticed that, for some speakers, the layers closer to the speech input were more correlated to arousal and the ones closer to the text output to valence. An example is shown in Figure 3. We present, in this section, preliminary studies regarding this matter.

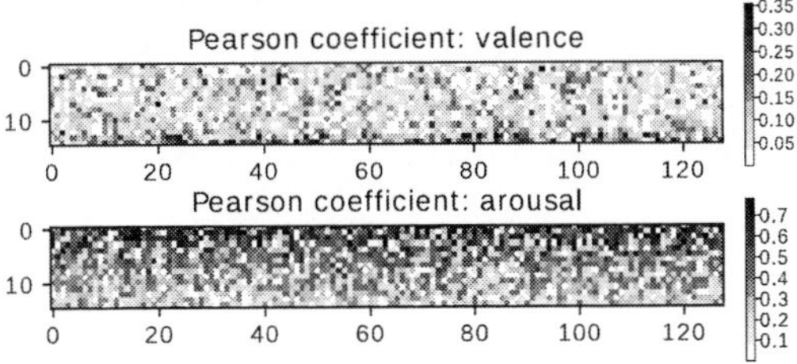

Figure 3: Pearson correlation coefficient between the neural features and valence (up) and arousal (down) - Female speaker of session 1

In order to analyze this phenomenon as precisely as possible, we only considered the utterances from the IEMOCAP database for which the valence/arousal annotators were consistent with each other, leaving us with 7532 utterances in total instead of 10039.

Then we performed linear regression with 4 different sets of feature to study their influence. For the first set, we select the 100 best features among the 3 first layers of the neural ASR in terms of Fisher score using scikit-learn. For the second set, we apply the same selection to the 3 last layers. The third set selection is applied among all neural features. The last set is the eGeMAPS feature set.

The results are summarized in Figure 2. As expected, the results show, that for the speakers considered, the layers closer to the audio modality outperform the ones closer to the text modality in the ASR architecture for arousal prediction and vice versa for the valence prediction. On this we build a hypothesis that the arousal-related features learned are more related to the audio modality than the text and vice versa for the valence-related features. This hypothesis will be further explored in future work.

4 Conclusions and Future work

In this paper, we show that features learned by a deep learning-based system trained for the Automatic Speech Recognition task can be used for emotion recognition and outperform the eGeMAPS feature set, the state of the art handcrafted features for emotion recognition. Then we investigate the correlation of the emotional dimensions arousal and valence with the modalities of audio and text of the speech. We show that for some speakers, arousal is more correlated to neural features extracted from layers closer to the speech modality and valence to the ones closer to the text modality.

To improve the system, we plan to perform an end-to-end training including the average operation. Another avenue to explore is to replace the average over time by a max-pooling over time which according to Aldeneh and Provost (2017) select the frames that are emotionally salient.

Then an analysis of the underlying activation evolutions could be done to see if it is possible to extract a frame-by-frame description of valence and arousal without having to annotate a database frame-by-frame.

Concerning the second experiment, we intend to investigate why these correlation patterns are only visible for some speakers and not others and the relationship between the arousal/valence and audio/text. We thereby hope to better understand the way multidimensional representations of emotions can be used to control the expressiveness in synthesized speech.

Acknowledgments

Noé Tits is funded through a PhD grant from the Fonds pour la Formation à la Recherche dans l'Industrie et l'Agriculture (FRIA), Belgium.

	Arousal		Valence	
	Mean	Variance	Mean	Variance
First layers	0.325	0.069	0.714	0.114
Last layers	0.357	0.038	0.661	0.089
All	0.296	0.044	0.621	0.099
eGeMAPS set	0.328	0.064	0.683	0.124

Table 2: Means and variances of the MSE on the prediction of valence and arousal.

References

Zakaria Aldeneh and Emily Mower Provost. 2017. Using regional saliency for speech emotion recognition. In *Acoustics, Speech and Signal Processing (ICASSP), 2017 IEEE International Conference on*, pages 2741–2745. IEEE.

Carlos Busso, Murtaza Bulut, Chi-Chun Lee, Abe Kazemzadeh, Emily Mower, Samuel Kim, Jeannette N Chang, Sungbok Lee, and Shrikanth S Narayanan. 2008. Iemocap: Interactive emotional dyadic motion capture database. *Language resources and evaluation*, 42(4):335.

Paul Ekman. 1992. An argument for basic emotions. *Cognition & emotion*, 6(3-4):169–200.

Florian Eyben, Klaus R Scherer, Björn W Schuller, Johan Sundberg, Elisabeth André, Carlos Busso, Laurence Y Devillers, Julien Epps, Petri Laukka, Shrikanth S Narayanan, et al. 2016. The geneva minimalistic acoustic parameter set (gemaps) for voice research and affective computing. *IEEE Transactions on Affective Computing*, 7(2):190–202.

Florian Eyben, Martin Wöllmer, and Björn Schuller. 2010. Opensmile: the munich versatile and fast open-source audio feature extractor. In *Proceedings of the 18th ACM international conference on Multimedia*, pages 1459–1462. ACM.

Jaebok Kim, Gwenn Englebienne, Khiet P. Truong, and Vanessa Evers. 2017a. Deep temporal models using identity skip-connections for speech emotion recognition. In *Proceedings of the 2017 ACM on Multimedia Conference*, MM '17, pages 1006–1013, New York, NY, USA. ACM.

Jaebok Kim, Gwenn Englebienne, Khiet P. Truong, and Vanessa Evers. 2017b. Towards speech emotion recognition "in the wild" using aggregated corpora and deep multi-task learning. In *INTERSPEECH*.

Ben Krause, Liang Lu, Iain Murray, and Steve Renals. 2016. Multiplicative lstm for sequence modelling. *arXiv preprint arXiv:1609.07959*.

Hector P Martinez, Yoshua Bengio, and Georgios N Yannakakis. 2013. Learning deep physiological models of affect. *IEEE Computational Intelligence Magazine*, 8(2):20–33.

Julian McAuley, Rahul Pandey, and Jure Leskovec. 2015. Inferring networks of substitutable and complementary products. In *Proceedings of the 21th ACM SIGKDD International Conference on Knowledge Discovery and Data Mining*, pages 785–794. ACM.

Brian McFee, Colin Raffel, Dawen Liang, Daniel PW Ellis, Matt McVicar, Eric Battenberg, and Oriol Nieto. 2015. librosa: Audio and music signal analysis in python. In *Proceedings of the 14th python in science conference*, pages 18–25.

Kim Namju and Park Kyubyong. 2016. Speech-to-text-wavenet. `https://github.com/buriburisuri/speech-to-text-wavenet`.

Sinno Jialin Pan and Qiang Yang. 2010. A survey on transfer learning. *IEEE Transactions on knowledge and data engineering*, 22(10):1345–1359.

F. Pedregosa, G. Varoquaux, A. Gramfort, V. Michel, B. Thirion, O. Grisel, M. Blondel, P. Prettenhofer, R. Weiss, V. Dubourg, J. Vanderplas, A. Passos, D. Cournapeau, M. Brucher, M. Perrot, and E. Duchesnay. 2011. Scikit-learn: Machine learning in Python. *Journal of Machine Learning Research*, 12:2825–2830.

Soujanya Poria, Erik Cambria, Devamanyu Hazarika, Navonil Majumder, Amir Zadeh, and Louis-Philippe Morency. 2017. Context-dependent sentiment analysis in user-generated videos. In *Proceedings of the 55th Annual Meeting of the Association for Computational Linguistics (Volume 1: Long Papers)*, volume 1, pages 873–883.

Alec Radford, Rafal Jozefowicz, and Ilya Sutskever. 2017. Learning to generate reviews and discovering sentiment. *arXiv preprint arXiv:1704.01444*.

James A Russell. 1980. A circumplex model of affect. *Journal of personality and social psychology*, 39(6):1161.

George Trigeorgis, Fabien Ringeval, Raymond Brueckner, Erik Marchi, Mihalis A Nicolaou, Björn Schuller, and Stefanos Zafeiriou. 2016. Adieu features? end-to-end speech emotion recognition using a deep convolutional recurrent network. In *Acoustics, Speech and Signal Processing (ICASSP), 2016 IEEE International Conference on*, pages 5200–5204. IEEE.

Aaron Van Den Oord, Sander Dieleman, Heiga Zen, Karen Simonyan, Oriol Vinyals, Alex Graves, Nal Kalchbrenner, Andrew Senior, and Koray Kavukcuoglu. 2016. Wavenet: A generative model for raw audio. *arXiv preprint arXiv:1609.03499*.

Christophe Veaux, Junichi Yamagishi, Kirsten MacDonald, et al. 2017. Cstr vctk corpus: English multi-speaker corpus for cstr voice cloning toolkit.

Amir Zadeh, Minghai Chen, Soujanya Poria, Erik Cambria, and Louis-Philippe Morency. 2017. Tensor fusion network for multimodal sentiment analysis. *arXiv preprint arXiv:1707.07250*.

Amir Zadeh, Paul Pu Liang, Navonil Mazumder, Soujanya Poria, Erik Cambria, and Louis-Philippe Morency. 2018. Memory fusion network for multi-view sequential learning. *arXiv preprint arXiv:1802.00927*.

Seq2Seq2Sentiment:
Multimodal Sequence to Sequence Models for Sentiment Analysis

Hai Pham[1], Thomas Manzini[1], Paul Pu Liang[2], Barnabás Poczós[2]
{[1]Language Technologies Institute, [2]Machine Learning Department}, CMU, USA
{htpham,tmanzini,pliang,bapoczos}@cs.cmu.edu

Abstract

Multimodal machine learning is a core research area spanning the language, visual and acoustic modalities. The central challenge in multimodal learning involves learning representations that can process and relate information from multiple modalities. In this paper, we propose two methods for unsupervised learning of joint multimodal representations using sequence to sequence (Seq2Seq) methods: a *Seq2Seq Modality Translation Model* and a *Hierarchical Seq2Seq Modality Translation Model*. We also explore multiple different variations on the multimodal inputs and outputs of these seq2seq models. Our experiments on multimodal sentiment analysis using the CMU-MOSI dataset indicate that our methods learn informative multimodal representations that outperform the baselines and achieve improved performance on multimodal sentiment analysis, specifically in the Bimodal case where our model is able to improve F1 Score by twelve points. We also discuss future directions for multimodal Seq2Seq methods.

1 Introduction

Sentiment analysis, which involves identifying a speaker's sentiment, is an open research problem. In this field, the majority of work done focused on unimodal methodologies - primarily textual analysis - where investigating was limited to identifying usage of words in positive and negative scenarios. However, unimodal textual sentiment analysis through usage of words, phrases, and their interdependencies were found to be insufficient for extracting affective content from textual opinions (Rosas et al., 2013).

As a result, there has been a recent push towards using statistical methods to extract additional behavioral cues not present in the language modality from the video and audio modalities. This research field is known as multimodal sentiment analysis and it extends the conventional text-based definition of sentiment analysis to a multimodal setup where different modalities contribute to modeling the sentiment of the speaker. For example, (Kaushik et al., 2013) explores modalities such as audio, while (Wöllmer et al., 2013) explores a multimodal approach to predicting sentiment. This push has been further bolstered by the advent of multimodal social media platforms, such as YouTube, Facebook, and VideoLectures which are used to express personal opinions on a worldwide scale. As a result, several multimodal datasets, such as CMU-MOSI (Zadeh et al., 2016) and later CMU-MOSEI (Zadeh et al., 2018c), ICT-MMMO (Wöllmer et al., 2013) and YouTube (Morency et al., 2011), take advantage of the abundance of multimodal data on the Internet. At the same time, neural network based multimodal models have been proposed that are highly effective at learning multimodal representations for multimodal sentiment analysis (Chen et al., 2017; Poria et al., 2017; Zadeh et al., 2018a,b).

Recent progress has been limited to supervised learning using labeled data, and does not take advantage of the abundant unlabeled data on the Internet. To address this gap, our work is primarily one of unsupervised representation learning. We attempt to learn a multimodal representation of our data in a structured paradigm and explore whether a joint multimodal representation trained via unsupervised learning can improve the performance for multimodal sentiment analysis. While representation learning has been an area of rapid research in the past years, there has been limited work that explores multimodal setting. To this end, we pro-

53

Proceedings of the First Grand Challenge and Workshop on Human Multimodal Language (Challenge-HML), pages 53–63,
Melbourne, Australia July 20, 2018. ©2018 Association for Computational Linguistics

pose two methods: a *Seq2Seq Modality Translation Model* and a *Hierarchical Seq2Seq Modality Translation Model* for unsupervised learning of multimodal representations. Our results show that using multimodal representations learned from our Seq2Seq modality translation method outperforms the baselines and achieves improved performance on multimodal sentiment analysis.

2 Related Work

In the past, approaches to text-based emotion and sentiment recognition rely mainly on rule-based techniques, bag of words (BoW) modeling or SNoW architecture (Chaumartin, 2007) using a large sentiment or emotion lexicon (Mishne et al., 2005), or statistical approaches that assume the availability of a large dataset annotated with polarity or emotion labels.

Multimodal sentiment analysis has gained a lot of research interests over the last few years (Baltrusaitis et al., 2017). Probably the most challenging task in multimodal sentiment analysis is to find a joint representation of multiple modalities. This problem is has been approached in a number of ways. Earlier works such as (Ngiam et al., 2011; Lazaridou et al., 2015; Kiros et al., 2014) have pushed some progress towards this direction.

Recently, more advanced neural network models were proposed to learn multimodal representations. The Multi-View LSTM (MV-LSTM) (Rajagopalan et al., 2016) was suggested to exploit fusion and temporal relationships. MV-LSTM partitions memory cells and gates into multiple regions corresponding to different views. Tensor Fusion Network (Zadeh et al., 2017) presented an efficient method based on Cartesian-product to take into consideration intramodal and intermodal relations between video, audio and text of the reviews to create a novel feature representation for each utterance. The Gated Multimodal Embedding model (Chen et al., 2017) created an algorithm using reinforcement learning to train an on-off switch that decided what values the video and audio components would have. Noisy modalities are turned off and clean modalities are allowed to pass through. (Zadeh et al., 2018a) utilizes external multimodal memory mechanisms to store multimodal information and create multimodal representations through time. (Zadeh et al., 2018b) proposed using multiple attention coefficient assignments to represent multiple cross-modal interactions. However, all these methods discussed so far are purely supervised approaches to multimodal sentiment analysis and do not leverage the power of unsupervised data and generative approaches towards learning multimodal representations.

Besides supervised approaches, generative methods based on generative adversarial networks (GAN) (Goodfellow et al., 2014) have attracted significant interest in learning joint distribution between two or more modalities (Donahue et al., 2016; Li et al., 2017; Gan et al., 2017). Another method to deal with multimodal problems is to view them as conditional problems which learn to map a modality to the other (Mirza and Osindero, 2014; Kingma et al., 2014; Pandey and Dukkipati, 2017). Our work can be viewed as an extension of the conditional approach, as both utilize unsupervised learning. However, our work differs from those in that it takes into account the sequential dependency within each modality.

Finally, attention based layers have also proved themselves to be effective tools to boost performance of neural network models, such as in neural machine translation (Klein et al.; Bahdanau et al., 2014; Luong et al., 2015), speech recognition (Sriram et al., 2017) and in image captioning (Xu et al., 2015). Our work also employs this mechanism in an attempt to better handle long-term dependencies of variable-length sequences.

3 Problem Formulation

Given a dataset with data $X = (X^{text}, X^{audio}, X^{video})$ where X^{text}, X^{audio}, X^{video} stand for text, audio and video modality inputs, respectively. Typically a dataset is indexed by videos. This means that if we have n videos, then $X = (X_1, X_2, ..., X_n)$ where $X_i = (X_i^{text}, X_i^{audio}, X_i^{video})$, $1 \le i \le n$. The corresponding labels for these n videos are $Y = (Y_1, Y_2, ..., Y_n)$, $Y_i \in \mathbb{R}$.

To simplify the problem, we align the input based on words. Typically, researchers often segment each video into a smaller set in which each segmented video will last a couple of seconds, instead of minutes as done in (Chen et al., 2017). After such alignment and segmentation, we have the equal-length inputs of each modality per video. For example, at the ith video, we have $X_i^{text} = (w_i^{(1)}, w_i^{(2)}, ..., w_i^{(T_i)})$ where $w_i^{(t)}$ stands for the tth word and T_i is the length of the ith video's text input, *a.k.a* time steps. Note that different videos will have different time steps. Similarly for this video, we have a sequence of audio input $X_i^{audio} = (a_i^{(1)}, a_i^{(2)}, ..., a_i^{(T_i)})$ and video input $X_i^{video} = (v_i^{(1)}, v_i^{(2)}, ..., v_i^{(T_i)})$.

In this work we are tackling the input learning problem where we want to learn the embedding representation for all text, audio, and video modalities: $\widetilde{X_i} = f(X_i) = f((X_i^{text}, X_i^{audio}, X_i^{video}))$. In our baseline model, the function f is simply the concatenation at time step level: $\widetilde{x}_i^t = [w_i^t; a_i^t; v_i^t]$

In our proposed method, we learn $\widetilde{X_i}$ by using a Seq2Seq model. We do not calculate each embedding representation for each time step, but for the whole sequence. Formally, $\widetilde{X_i} = f(X_i) = Seq2Seq\_Encoder(X_i)$ where $Seq2Seq\_Encoder$ is the encoder part of our Seq2Seq model.

Now, we have the transformed inputs $\widetilde{X} = (\widetilde{X_1}, \widetilde{X_2}, ..., \widetilde{X_n})$ and outputs $Y = (Y_1, Y_2, ..., Y_n)$ for n videos, where $\widetilde{X_i} = (\widetilde{x}_i^1, \widetilde{x}_i^2, ..., \widetilde{x}_i^{T_i})$. For simplicity, in the next formula, we omit the index of video segment i, and so the input becomes $\widetilde{X} = (\widetilde{x}^1, \widetilde{x}^2, ..., \widetilde{x}^T)$, and the labels become $Y = (y^1, y^2, ..., y^T)$.

We will be using a Recurrent Neural Network (RNN) such as LSTM (Hochreiter and Schmidhuber, 1997) or GRU (Chung et al., 2015) to model this sequence. In detail, this RNN has a stack of K hidden layers $h = (h^1, h^2, ..., h^K)$, each contains D hidden neurons: $h^k = (h_1^k, h_2^k, ..., h_D^k)$, $k \in [1, K]$. We denote W and b to be weight and bias, then for the first layer which contacts directly with input:

$$h^1{}_t = H(W_{xh^1}\widetilde{x}_t + W_{h^1h^1}h^1{}_{t-1} + b_{h^1}) \qquad (1)$$

where H is the RNN cell function. For example of LSTM, it contains *input, forget, output* and *cell state*. At hidden layer $k \in [2, K]$:

$$h^k{}_t = H(W_{h^{t-1}h^t}h_t^{k-1} + W_{h^kh^k}h^k{}_{t-1} + b_{h^k}) \qquad (2)$$

Optionally, we apply a soft attention mechanism *on top* of the last hidden layer h^K, with shared weight W_α over T time steps, then we can obtain the attention output α:

$$\alpha = softmax\left(\begin{bmatrix} W_\alpha h_1^K \\ W_\alpha h_2^K \\ ... \\ W_\alpha h_T^K \end{bmatrix}\right) \qquad (3)$$

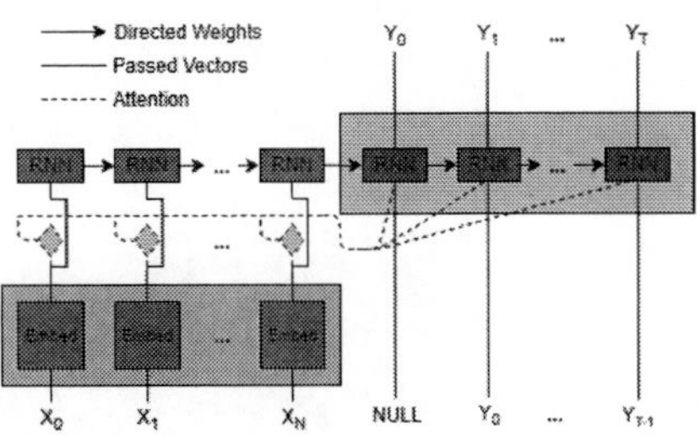

Figure 1: Seq2Seq Modality Translation Model with input $(X_1, ..., X_N)$ and output is $(Y_1, ..., Y_T)$. Seq2Seq makes use of the whole input sequence in the decoding phase for every token Y_i. If attention model (yellow color) is used, for each Y_i, it learns a separate weight vector *w.r.t* each token of input X to see which token should the decoder "attend" more.

The last hidden layer's output now becomes:

$$A = [h_1^K, h_2^K, ..., h_T^K]\alpha = H^K\alpha \qquad (4)$$

And the last output layer with regression score is:

$$\widetilde{y}_t = W_{Ay}A + b_y \qquad (5)$$

Finally, we calculate the loss with respect to the labels. As in (Chen et al., 2017), we choose Mean Absolute Error (MAE) as our loss and later train with stochastic gradient descent:

$$\mathbb{L}_{MAE}(\widetilde{Y}, Y) = \mathbb{E}[|\widetilde{Y} - Y|] \qquad (6)$$

4 Proposed Approach

In this section we describe the different approaches that we plan to take to improve affect recognition through learning multimodal representations.

4.1 Seq2Seq Modality Translation Model

The *Seq2Seq Modality Translation Model* aims to learn multimodal representations that can be used for discriminative tasks. While Seq2Seq models have been predominantly used for machine translation (Bahdanau et al., 2014; Luong et al., 2015), we extend its usage to the realm of multimodal machine learning where we use it to translate one modality to another, or translate a joint representation to another single or joint representation. To do so, we propose a Seq2Seq modality translation model with attention mechanism, as shown in Figure 1. Modality X is translated into modality Y. Our hypothesis is that the intermediate representation of this model, i.e. the output of Seq2Seq's encoder, or the input of its decoder, is close to the joint representation (X, Y) of the two modalities

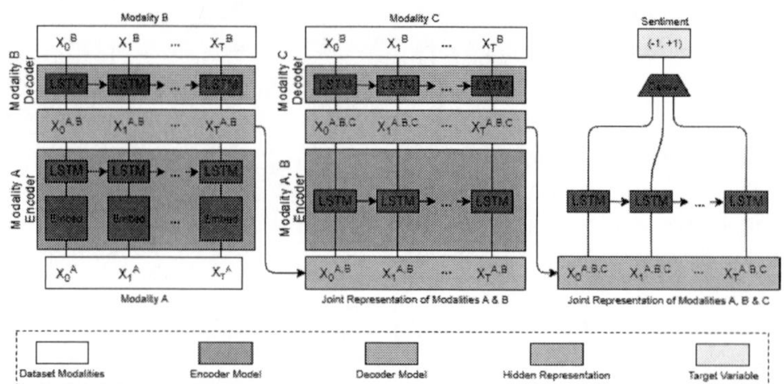

Figure 2: Hierarchical Seq2Seq Modality Translation Model: first we train with 2 modalities, then we add one more on the second phase, from which the results will be fed into RNN for sentiment prediction. The green boxes denote the joint representation learned by Seq2Seq models: the joint representation of modalities A and B will be fed into another Seq2Seq model which in turn learns the joint representation of AB and another modality C. Finally the joint representation of ABC will be fed into a RNN to predict sentiment.

involved. As a result, this representation can be used for tasks that involve learning joint representation across multiple modalities. The detail is in Algorithm 1.

Algorithm 1 Seq2Seq Modality Translation

X, Y, S are 2 modalities and sentiment sequences

1: **Phase 1: Train Seq2Seq**
2:    $\mathcal{E}_{XY} \leftarrow Seq2Seq\_RNN\_Encode(X)$
3:    $\widetilde{Y} \leftarrow Seq2Seq\_RNN\_Decode(\mathcal{E}_{XY})$
4:    $loss = cross\_entropy(\widetilde{Y}, Y)$
5:    Backprop to update params

6: **Phase 2: Sentiment Regression**
7:    $\mathcal{E}_{XY} \leftarrow Seq2Seq\_RNN\_Encode(X)$ $\triangleright$ trained encoder in Seq2Seq model
8:    $R = RNN(\mathcal{E}_{XY})$
9:    $score \leftarrow Regression(R)$
10:    $loss \leftarrow MAE(score, S)$
11:    Backprop to update params

Formally, the Seq2Seq Modality Translation Model consists of 2 separate steps: encoding and decoding, each phase typically consists of a single RNN or a stack of them. This model accepts variable-length inputs of X and Y, and the network should be trained to maximize the translational condition probability $p(Y|X)$. For encoding, it encodes the whole input sequence X into an embedded representation. The hidden state output of each time step is based on the previous hidden state along with the input sequence (refer to Figure 1):

$$h_n = RNN(h_{n-1}, X_n) \qquad (7)$$

The encoder's output is the final hidden state's output of the encoding RNN:

$$\mathcal{E} = h_N = RNN(h_{N-1}, X_N) \qquad (8)$$

where N is the length of the input sequence X. The decoder tries to decode each token Y_i at a time based on $\mathcal{E}$ and all previous decoded tokens, which is formulated as:

$$p(Y) = \prod_{i=1}^{T} p(Y_i|\mathcal{E}, Y_1, ..., Y_{i-1}) \qquad (9)$$

The Seq2Seq training target is to find the best translation sequence which is as close to the ground truth Y as possible, or formally:

$$\widehat{Y} = \arg\max_{Y} p(Y|X) \qquad (10)$$

And while there are some other search algorithms such as random sampling or greedy search to decode each token (Neubig, 2017), we use the traditional beam search approach (Sutskever et al., 2014).

4.2 Hierarchical Seq2Seq Modality Translation Model

The Seq2Seq Modality Translation Model only learns joint representation between 2 modalities X and Y. While this might be a strong starting point, we believe an approach that captures the joint interactions between all different modalities X, Y, Z is more effective in modeling the full distribution of the multimodal data and therefore more useful for regression or classification. In response, we propose the *Hierarchical Seq2Seq Modality Translation Model* that learns a joint multimodal representation. Once the Seq2Seq Modality Translation Model is trained for 2 modalities X and Y, we obtain the intermediate representation $\mathcal{E}_{XY}$ which is the joint representation of (X, Y). $\mathcal{E}_{XY}$

is in turn treated as input sequence for the next Seq2Seq Modality Translation Model to decode the third modality Z. The final multimodal representation $\mathcal{E}_{XYZ}$ represents the joint representation of (X, Y, Z). The Hierarchical Seq2Seq Modality Translation Model is described as in Algorithm 2.

Algorithm 2 Hierarchical Seq2Seq Modality Translation: X, Y, Z, S are 3 modalities and sentiment sequences

---

1: **Phase 1: Train Seq2Seq for 2 modalities**
2:   $\mathcal{E}_{XY} \leftarrow Seq2Seq\_RNN\_Encode(X)$
3:   $\widetilde{Y} \leftarrow Seq2Seq\_RNN\_Decode(\mathcal{E}_{XY})$
4:   $loss = cross\_entropy(\widetilde{Y}, Y)$
5:   Backpropagate to update parameters

6: **Phase 2: Train Seq2Seq for 3 modalities**
7:   $\mathcal{E}_{XYZ} \leftarrow Seq2Seq\_RNN\_Encode(\mathcal{E}_{XY})$
8:   $\widetilde{Z} \leftarrow Seq2Seq\_RNN\_Decode(\mathcal{E}_{XYZ})$
9:   $loss = cross\_entropy(\widetilde{Z}, Z)$
10:   Backpropagate to update parameters

11: **Phase 3: Sentiment Regression**
12:   $\mathcal{E}_{XYZ} \leftarrow Seq2Seq\_RNN\_Encode(\mathcal{E}_{XY})$
13:   $R = RNN(\mathcal{E}_{XYZ})$
14:   $score \leftarrow Regression(R)$
15:   $loss \leftarrow MAE(score, S)$
16:   Backpropagate to update parameters

This strategy is also illustrated in Figure 2. The output of the second Seq2Seq model is the input of the last RNN model where we will train to predict regression sentiment scores. This last Seq2Seq model will be trained using MAE loss function and it perform subsequent regression process.

5 Experimental Setup

We explored the applications of this model to the CMU-MOSI dataset (Zadeh et al., 2016). We implemented a baseline LSTM model based off the work done in (Chen et al., 2017). Our implementation uses 66.67% of the data for training from which we take a 15.15% held-out set for validation, and the remaining 33.33% is used for testing. Finally, we evaluated our proposed model against the baseline results generated by the implementation of (Chen et al., 2017). Here we compared our results against the various multimodal configurations evaluating our performance using precision, recall, and F1 scores.

5.1 Dataset and Input Modalities

The dataset that we use to explore applications of our model is the CMU Multimodal Opinion-level Sentiment Intensity dataset (CMU-MOSI). The dataset contains video, audio, and transcriptions of 89 different speakers in 93 different videos divided into 2199 separate opinion sentiments. Each video has an associated sentiment label in the range from -3 to 3. The low end of the spectrum (-3) indicates strongly negative sentiment, where as the high end of the spectrum indicates strongly positive sentiment (+3), and ratings of 0 indicate neutral sentiment. The CMU-MOSI dataset is currently subject to much research (Poria et al., 2017; Chen et al., 2017; Zadeh et al., 2018a,b) and the current state of the art is achieved by (Poria et al., 2017) with an F1 score of 80.3 using a context aware model across entire videos. The state of the art using only individual segments is achieved by (Zadeh et al., 2018a) with an F1 score of 77.3.

With respect to raw features that are being given as inputs to our model, we perform feature extraction in the same manner as described in (Chen et al., 2017). In the text domain, pretrained 300 dimensional GLoVe embeddings (Pennington et al., 2014) were used to represent the textual tokens. In the audio domain, low level acoustic features including 12 Mel-frequency cepstral coefficients (MFCCs), pitch tracking and voiced/unvoiced segmenting features (Drugman and Alwan, 2011), glottal source parameters (Childers and Lee, 1991; Drugman et al., 2012; Alku, 1992; Alku et al., 1997, 2002), peak slope parameters and maxima dispersion quotients (Kane and Gobl, 2013) were extracted automatically using COVAREP (Degottex et al., 2014). Finally, in the video domain, Facet (iMotions, 2017) is used to extract per-frame basic and advanced emotions and facial action units as indicators of facial muscle movement (Ekman, 1992; Ekman et al., 1980).

In situations where the same time alignment between different modalities are required, we choose the granularity of the input to be at the level of words. The words are aligned with audio using P2FA (Yuan and Liberman, 2008) to get their exact utterance times. The visual and acoustic modalities are aligned to words using these utterance times.

5.2 Baselines

We use a LSTM model implemented in 3 different ways (one for each different grouping of the modalities). First in the unimodal domain, we run sentiment regression based solely on one modality, second in the bimodal domain we change the input to the concatenation of any pair of modality, and

Method	Feature	BINARY (−1, +1)			7-CLASS (−3, ..., +3)		
		Prec	Recall	F1	Prec	Recall	F1
UniModal-Baseline	Text (T)	**0.77**	**0.76**	**0.76**	**0.32**	**0.35**	**0.33**
	Audio (A)	0.56	0.56	0.56	0.12	0.19	0.14
	Video (V)	0.57	0.47	0.48	0.12	0.19	0.12

Table 1: Unimodal baseline results with 3 metrics: Precision, Recall and F-Score (F1)

finally in the trimodal domain we concatenate all three modalities. This baseline not only serves to act as a benchmark for comparing our results but also acts as a starting point for our code development. As such, any improvements in our metrics are strictly as a result of the representations that we have learned and not structural changes in our model.

5.3 Multimodal Model Variations

Throughout our experimentation, we apply the algorithms in Section 4 with several intuitive variations of how to translate modalities. Below are all approaches that we try to maximize our chances of learning a strong representation.

For bimodal, we translate one modality into another one. For example, A → V stands for translating from Audio to Video, and take the embedding state, which we refer to as embed(A+V), to predict sentiment. Here we employ the Seq2Seq Modality Translation Model mentioned in Algorithm 1.

For trimodal, there are a lot more variations as follows. First, since we have 3 different modality and Seq2Seq is only capable of translating one modality to another, we use the Hierarchical Seq2Seq Modality Translation Model which is mentioned in Algorithm 2, e.g. we translate from T to A to have the joint representation embed(T+A), and then continue the translation from embed(T+A) to the rest modality which is V, which in turn yields the joint representation embed(T+A+V) to make sentiment prediction.

Second, we reuse the previous Seq2Seq Modality Translation Model to translate a concatenation of 2 modality to the rest, e.g. concat(T+V) to A, and vice versa, e.g. translating from A back to concat(T+V).

Finally, we still use the Seq2Seq Modality Translation Model to translate from a concatenation of 2 modality to another concatenation of other 2. With this setting, at least one modality is repeated, and base on many previous works and our experience, we tend to favor text modality (T) over the other two and make it repeated.

6 Results

6.1 Baseline Unimodal Results

We see that with the baseline model, as shown Table 1, the text modality is by far the most discriminative when it comes to detecting emotion. This implies that users rely heavily on their word choice and language to convey meaning and emotion. While this may be true, we know that other works such as (Zadeh et al., 2018a; Poria et al., 2017) have achieved higher scores by combining all these different modalities. This implies that with some careful thinking and pointed model construction, we should be able to improve upon our baseline unimodal results through the integration of additional modalities into our model.

6.2 Baseline Multimodal Results

The results of our different baseline multimodal approaches is shown in Table 2 for bimodal and Table 3 for trimodal. We see that of the multimodal baselines the model which combines the 3 modalities of text, speech, and video performed the best. The baseline model which combined text and audio arrived in second place followed closely by the combined text and video model. The model which combines video and audio arrived in last place by a significant margin. This corroborates our results from our unimodal baselines which implied that the text modality is the most discriminative modality in this dataset.

On the whole we can see that when all three modalities are working in concert we get the best result in a multimodal context, however, it is worth noting that we were not able to match out unimodal baseline with our multimodal models. This implies that there is still more to be drawn from our data when constructing our model and there is generally more work to be done. We believe that incorporating a stronger more robust representation of our data will be beneficial to our later attempts at classification. Though we view this to be out of scope of this work as the focus of this work is on learning informative representations.

Method	Feature	BINARY (−1, +1)			7-CLASS (−3, ..., +3)		
		Prec	Recall	F1	Prec	Recall	F1
BiModal-Baseline	concat(T + V)	**0.78**	**0.67**	0.55	0.01	0.16	0.05
	concat(T + A)	0.44	0.66	0.53	0.02	0.15	0.04
	concat(A + V)	0.55	0.47	0.48	0.13	0.16	0.11
BiModal-Seq2Seq	T → V	0.67	**0.67**	**0.67**	0.26	0.22	**0.22**
	T → A	0.66	0.64	0.65	**0.28**	0.24	0.18
	A → T	0.55	0.60	0.56	0.17	**0.34**	0.11
	A → V	0.55	0.55	0.54	0.16	0.18	0.16
	V → T	0.58	0.58	0.58	0.05	0.16	0.08
	V → A	0.58	0.62	0.58	0.12	0.17	0.01

Table 2: Bimodal results with 3 metrics: Precision, Recall and F-Score (F1)

Method	Feature	BINARY (−1, +1)			7-CLASS (−3, ..., +3)		
		Prec	Recall	F1	Prec	Recall	F1
TriModal-Baseline	concat(T + V + A)	**0.75**	**0.75**	**0.75**	0.24	**0.27**	**0.24**
TriModal-Seq2Seq	embed(T, V) → A	0.56	0.60	0.57	0.10	0.16	0.09
	embed(T, A) → V	0.60	0.55	0.56	0.26	0.15	0.07
	embed(A, V) → T	0.66	0.53	0.44	0.16	0.04	0.09
	embed(A, T) → V	0.59	0.51	0.52	0.13	0.15	0.09
	embed(V, T) → A	0.59	0.60	0.59	0.11	0.17	0.10
	embed(V, A) → T	0.57	0.61	0.58	0.11	0.17	0.09
	concat(T, V) → A	0.67	0.66	0.65	0.22	0.17	0.18
	concat(A, T) → V	0.54	0.55	0.63	0.19	0.15	0.21
	concat(V, A) → T	0.59	0.59	0.58	0.16	0.12	0.12
	T → concat(A, V)	0.70	0.65	0.66	0.23	0.22	0.18
	A → concat(T, V)	0.55	0.53	0.54	0.18	0.20	0.18
	concat(T, A) → concat(T, V)	0.62	0.60	0.61	0.23	0.24	0.22
	concat(T, V) → concat(T, A)	0.68	0.70	0.67	**0.31**	0.24	0.19

Table 3: Trimodal results with 3 metrics: Precision, Recall and F-Score (F1)

6.3 Analysis of Baseline Failure Cases

The common trend that we see among all of those baseline models is the consistent failure to identify extreme cases of either positive or negative emotions. We believe that this phenomenon is due to two possibilities. First we see that there are very few cases of highly positive (+3) and highly negative (−3) examples in the training data. As a result the models that are trained are highly biased towards not selecting +3 or −3 ratings. Secondly, our baseline models are performing categorical classification as opposed to regression or ordinal classification. We plan to solve by training the model to perform this type of prediction as a regression task as opposed to a categorical classification task.

6.4 Bimodal Seq2Seq Results

Our bimodal models require the exploration of two modalities, one for the encoding step and another for the decoding step. We explored several different different encoder/decoder frameworks for these models. The first model that we explored were representations generated from encoding exactly one modality and then decoding exactly one dif-ferent modality. The results of this approach are included below in Table 2. Here we can see that the Seq2Seq Modality Translation Model outperforms the baseline method in terms of F1 consistently and outperforms in terms of precision and recall in several cases, but not all.

6.5 Trimodal Seq2Seq Results

We try all variations mentioned in Section 5.3 and the full breakdown of these results can be found in the Table 3. According to that, while the Hierarchical Seq2Seq Modality Translation Model is a natural extension to the normal Seq2Seq Modality Translation model, it does not perform well on the CMU-MOSI dataset. Otherwise, using the normal non-hierarchical model with concatenation variations does improve the performance, and particularly beats the baseline (for only F1 score) on the model which translates from concat(T,V) to concat(T+A) for the 7-class case. As mentioned in Section 5.3, we favor the text (T) modality and make it repeated in this setting because it typically contributes more significantly to sentiment prediction. Indeed, we have tried to repeat video or audio modality but the result shrinks dramatically.

One possible reason for this behavior is the scarcity of training data. Given that at every phase of Seq2Seq translation, we only have 1289 train samples, 230 validation and 269 test samples, Seq2Seq, which typically requires more data for training a good model, does not work efficiently. This affects even more in the hierarchical Seq2Seq cases where we train two phases of Seq2Seq. We project the performance will improve if we work on other dataset which is bigger, or if we pretrain our model on other dataset first before applying it to MOSI.

7 Discussion

The language modality is the most discriminative as well as the most important towards learning multimodal representations. While we outperform the baseline multimodal approach we were unable to outperform the baseline unimodal text approach. Clearly from these results we know that that the text modality is the most discriminative of all of these modalities. However, it appears that these models which we have described are not able to truly separate the importance of the text modality. The fact that we are merging these modalities into a shared representation space is likely decreasing the resolution of the text domain and thus decreasing the modeling power of the domain. This is why we believe that the top performing multimodal model is one that incorporates the text domain so much (see Tables 2 and 3).

It is worth noting that some of the learned representations were quite poor when it came to their use in prediction. For example, representations that were learned using only audio and video generally performed poorly. This is to be expected given the already known information that these modalities are not as discriminative as the language modality. At the same time, some of the worse performing representations were learned in the methodology of learning a representation based on an existing embedding. We believe this to be due to the representation losing the resolution of the original two domains from which the original source embedding was learned and instead being focused on learning the best representation to predict the final modality.

8 Future Directions

This research opens up a promising direction in joint unsupervised learning of multimodal repre-

sentations and supervised learning of multimodal temporal data. We propose the following extensions that could improve performance:

Firstly, using an Variational Autoencoder (VAE) (Kingma and Welling, 2013) in conjunction with LSTM Encoder/Decoder model (as in the case of VAE Seq2Seq model) would be an interesting avenue to explore. This is because VAEs have been shown to learn better representations as compared to vanilla autoencoders (Kingma and Welling, 2013; Pu et al., 2016).

Secondly, since our method for multimodal representation learning is unsupervised, we could take advantage of larger external datasets to pre-train the multimodal representations before fine-tuning further with CMU-MOSI. We believe this will boost performance because we have limited data in CMU-MOSI for training (CMU-MOSI has 2199 training segments). Some datasets that come to mind include the Persuasion Opinion Multimodal (POM) dataset (Park et al., 2014) with 1000 total videos (longer than segments) and the IEMOCAP dataset with 10000 total segment. Since these datasets also consist of monologue speaker videos, we expect the learnt multimodal representations to generalize.

Thirdly, our method does not train our combined model end to end: the representations that we use to generated during on training run and the sentiment classification model are trained separately. Exploring an end-to-end version of this model end to end could possibly result in better performance where we could additionally fine tune the learned multimodal representation for sentiment analysis.

9 Conclusion

To conclude, this paper investigate the problem of multimodal representation learning to leverage the abundance of unlabeled multimedia data available on the internet. We presente two methods for unsupervised learning of joint multimodal representations using multimodal Seq2Seq models: the *Seq2Seq Modality Translation Model* and the *Hierarchical Seq2Seq Modality Translation Model*. We found that these intermediate multimodal representations can then be used for multimodal downstream tasks. Our experiments indicate that the multimodal representations learned from our Seq2Seq modality translation method are highly informative and achieves improved performance on multimodal sentiment analysis.

References

Paavo Alku. 1992. Glottal wave analysis with pitch synchronous iterative adaptive inverse filtering. *Speech communication* 11(2-3):109–118.

Paavo Alku, Tom Bäckström, and Erkki Vilkman. 2002. Normalized amplitude quotient for parametrization of the glottal flow. *the Journal of the Acoustical Society of America* 112(2):701–710.

Paavo Alku, Helmer Strik, and Erkki Vilkman. 1997. Parabolic spectral parameter - a new method for quantification of the glottal flow. *Speech Communication* 22(1):67–79.

Dzmitry Bahdanau, Kyunghyun Cho, and Yoshua Bengio. 2014. Neural machine translation by jointly learning to align and translate. *arXiv preprint arXiv:1409.0473* .

Tadas Baltrusaitis, Chaitanya Ahuja, and Louis-Philippe Morency. 2017. Multimodal machine learning: A survey and taxonomy. *CoRR* abs/1705.09406. http://arxiv.org/abs/1705.09406.

François-Régis Chaumartin. 2007. Upar7: A knowledge-based system for headline sentiment tagging. In *Proceedings of the 4th International Workshop on Semantic Evaluations*. Association for Computational Linguistics, Stroudsburg, PA, USA, SemEval '07, pages 422–425. http://dl.acm.org/citation.cfm?id=1621474.1621568.

Minghai Chen, Sen Wang, Paul Pu Liang, Tadas Baltrusaitis, Amir Zadeh, and Morency Louis-Phillipe. 2017. Multimodal sentiment analysis with word-level fusion and reinforcement learning. *ICMI, Glassgow, United Kingdom* .

Donald G Childers and CK Lee. 1991. Vocal quality factors: Analysis, synthesis, and perception. *the Journal of the Acoustical Society of America* 90(5):2394–2410.

Junyoung Chung, Caglar Gulcehre, Kyunghyun Cho, and Yoshua Bengio. 2015. Gated feedback recurrent neural networks. In *International Conference on Machine Learning*. pages 2067–2075.

Gilles Degottex, John Kane, Thomas Drugman, Tuomo Raitio, and Stefan Scherer. 2014. Covarep - a collaborative voice analysis repository for speech technologies. In *Acoustics, Speech and Signal Processing (ICASSP), 2014 IEEE International Conference on*. IEEE, pages 960–964.

Jeff Donahue, Philipp Krähenbühl, and Trevor Darrell. 2016. Adversarial feature learning. *arXiv preprint arXiv:1605.09782* .

Thomas Drugman and Abeer Alwan. 2011. Joint robust voicing detection and pitch estimation based on residual harmonics. In *Interspeech*. pages 1973–1976.

Thomas Drugman, Mark Thomas, Jon Gudnason, Patrick Naylor, and Thierry Dutoit. 2012. Detection of glottal closure instants from speech signals: A quantitative review. *IEEE Transactions on Audio, Speech, and Language Processing* 20(3):994–1006.

Paul Ekman. 1992. An argument for basic emotions. *Cognition & emotion* 6(3-4):169–200.

Paul Ekman, Wallace V Freisen, and Sonia Ancoli. 1980. Facial signs of emotional experience. *Journal of personality and social psychology* 39(6):1125.

Zhe Gan, Liqun Chen, Weiyao Wang, Yunchen Pu, Yizhe Zhang, Hao Liu, Chunyuan Li, and Lawrence Carin. 2017. Triangle generative adversarial networks. *arXiv preprint arXiv:1709.06548* .

Ian Goodfellow, Jean Pouget-Abadie, Mehdi Mirza, Bing Xu, David Warde-Farley, Sherjil Ozair, Aaron Courville, and Yoshua Bengio. 2014. Generative adversarial nets. In *Advances in neural information processing systems*. pages 2672–2680.

Sepp Hochreiter and Jürgen Schmidhuber. 1997. Long short-term memory. *Neural computation* 9(8):1735–1780.

iMotions. 2017. Facial expression analysis. goo.gl/1rh1JN.

John Kane and Christer Gobl. 2013. Wavelet maxima dispersion for breathy to tense voice discrimination. *IEEE Transactions on Audio, Speech, and Language Processing* 21(6):1170–1179.

Lakshmish Kaushik, Abhijeet Sangwan, and John HL Hansen. 2013. Sentiment extraction from natural audio streams. In *Acoustics, speech and signal processing (icassp), 2013 ieee international conference on*. IEEE, pages 8485–8489.

Diederik P Kingma, Shakir Mohamed, Danilo Jimenez Rezende, and Max Welling. 2014. Semi-supervised learning with deep generative models. In *Advances in Neural Information Processing Systems*. pages 3581–3589.

Diederik P Kingma and Max Welling. 2013. Auto-encoding variational bayes. *arXiv preprint arXiv:1312.6114* .

Ryan Kiros, Ruslan Salakhutdinov, and Richard S Zemel. 2014. Unifying visual-semantic embeddings with multimodal neural language models. *arXiv preprint arXiv:1411.2539* .

G. Klein, Y. Kim, Y. Deng, J. Senellart, and A. M. Rush. ????. OpenNMT: Open-Source Toolkit for Neural Machine Translation. *ArXiv e-prints* .

Angeliki Lazaridou, Nghia The Pham, and Marco Baroni. 2015. Combining language and vision with a multimodal skip-gram model. *arXiv preprint arXiv:1501.02598* .

Chongxuan Li, Kun Xu, Jun Zhu, and Bo Zhang. 2017. Triple generative adversarial nets. *arXiv preprint arXiv:1703.02291* .

Minh-Thang Luong, Hieu Pham, and Christopher D Manning. 2015. Effective approaches to attention-based neural machine translation. *arXiv preprint arXiv:1508.04025* .

Mehdi Mirza and Simon Osindero. 2014. Conditional generative adversarial nets. *arXiv preprint arXiv:1411.1784* .

Gilad Mishne et al. 2005. Experiments with mood classification in blog posts. In *Proceedings of ACM SIGIR 2005 workshop on stylistic analysis of text for information access*. volume 19, pages 321–327.

Louis-Philippe Morency, Rada Mihalcea, and Payal Doshi. 2011. Towards multimodal sentiment analysis: Harvesting opinions from the web. In *Proceedings of the 13th international conference on multimodal interfaces*. ACM, pages 169–176.

Graham Neubig. 2017. Neural machine translation and sequence-to-sequence models: A tutorial. *arXiv preprint arXiv:1703.01619* .

Jiquan Ngiam, Aditya Khosla, Mingyu Kim, Juhan Nam, Honglak Lee, and Andrew Y Ng. 2011. Multimodal deep learning. In *Proceedings of the 28th international conference on machine learning (ICML-11)*. pages 689–696.

Gaurav Pandey and Ambedkar Dukkipati. 2017. Variational methods for conditional multimodal deep learning. In *Neural Networks (IJCNN), 2017 International Joint Conference on*. IEEE, pages 308–315.

Sunghyun Park, Han Suk Shim, Moitreya Chatterjee, Kenji Sagae, and Louis-Philippe Morency. 2014. Computational analysis of persuasiveness in social multimedia: A novel dataset and multimodal prediction approach. In *Proceedings of the 16th International Conference on Multimodal Interaction*. ACM, New York, NY, USA, ICMI '14, pages 50–57. https://doi.org/10.1145/2663204.2663260.

Jeffrey Pennington, Richard Socher, and Christopher D Manning. 2014. Glove: Global vectors for word representation. In *EMNLP*. volume 14, pages 1532–1543.

Soujanya Poria, Erik Cambria, Devamanyu Hazarika, Navonil Majumder, Amir Zadeh, and Louis-Philippe Morency. 2017. Context-dependent sentiment analysis in user-generated videos. In *Proceedings of the 55th Annual Meeting of the Association for Computational Linguistics (Volume 1: Long Papers)*. volume 1, pages 873–883.

Yunchen Pu, Zhe Gan, Ricardo Henao, Xin Yuan, Chunyuan Li, Andrew Stevens, and Lawrence Carin. 2016. Variational autoencoder for deep learning of images, labels and captions. In D. D. Lee,

M. Sugiyama, U. V. Luxburg, I. Guyon, and R. Garnett, editors, *Advances in Neural Information Processing Systems 29*, Curran Associates, Inc., pages 2352–2360.

Shyam Sundar Rajagopalan, Louis-Philippe Morency, Tadas Baltrusaitis, and Roland Goecke. 2016. *Extending Long Short-Term Memory for Multi-View Structured Learning*, Springer International Publishing, Cham, pages 338–353.

Verónica Pérez Rosas, Rada Mihalcea, and Louis-Philippe Morency. 2013. Multimodal sentiment analysis of spanish online videos. *IEEE Intelligent Systems* 28(3):38–45.

Anuroop Sriram, Heewoo Jun, Sanjeev Satheesh, and Adam Coates. 2017. Cold fusion: Training seq2seq models together with language models. *arXiv preprint arXiv:1708.06426* .

Ilya Sutskever, Oriol Vinyals, and Quoc V Le. 2014. Sequence to sequence learning with neural networks. In *Advances in neural information processing systems*. pages 3104–3112.

Martin Wöllmer, Felix Weninger, Tobias Knaup, Björn Schuller, Congkai Sun, Kenji Sagae, and Louis-Philippe Morency. 2013. Youtube movie reviews: Sentiment analysis in an audio-visual context. *IEEE Intelligent Systems* 28(3):46–53.

Kelvin Xu, Jimmy Ba, Ryan Kiros, Kyunghyun Cho, Aaron Courville, Ruslan Salakhudinov, Rich Zemel, and Yoshua Bengio. 2015. Show, attend and tell: Neural image caption generation with visual attention. In *International Conference on Machine Learning*. pages 2048–2057.

Jiahong Yuan and Mark Liberman. 2008. Speaker identification on the scotus corpus. *Journal of the Acoustical Society of America* 123(5):3878.

Amir Zadeh, Minghai Chen, Soujanya Poria, Erik Cambria, and Louis-Philippe Morency. 2017. Tensor fusion network for multimodal sentiment analysis. In *Proceedings of the 2017 Conference on Empirical Methods in Natural Language Processing*. pages 1114–1125.

Amir Zadeh, Paul Pu Liang, Navonil Mazumder, Soujanya Poria, Erik Cambria, and Louis-Philippe Morency. 2018a. Memory fusion network for multi-view sequential learning. *arXiv preprint arXiv:1802.00927* .

Amir Zadeh, Paul Pu Liang, Soujanya Poria, Prateek Vij, Erik Cambria, and Louis-Philippe Morency. 2018b. Multi-attention recurrent network for human communication comprehension. *arXiv preprint arXiv:1802.00923* .

Amir Zadeh, Paul Pu Liang, Jon Vanbriesen, Soujanya Poria, Erik Cambria, Minghai Chen, and Louis-Philippe Morency. 2018c. Multimodal language analysis in the wild: Cmu-mosei dataset and interpretable dynamic fusion graph. In *Association for Computational Linguistics (ACL)*.

Amir Zadeh, Rowan Zellers, Eli Pincus, and Louis-Philippe Morency. 2016. Multimodal sentiment intensity analysis in videos: Facial gestures and verbal messages. *IEEE Intelligent Systems* 31(6):82–88.

DNN Multimodal Fusion Techniques for Predicting Video Sentiment

Jennifer Williams, Ramona Comanescu, Oana Radu, and Leimin Tian
Centre for Speech Technology Research (CSTR)
University of Edinburgh, UK
j.williams@ed.ac.uk

Abstract

We present our work on sentiment prediction using the benchmark MOSI dataset from the CMU-MultimodalDataSDK. Previous work on multimodal sentiment analysis have been focused on input-level feature fusion or decision-level fusion for multimodal fusion. Here, we propose an intermediate-level feature fusion, which merges weights from each modality (audio, video, and text) during training with subsequent additional training. Moreover, we tested principle component analysis (PCA) for feature selection. We found that applying PCA increases unimodal performance, and multimodal fusion outperforms unimodal models. Our experiments show that our proposed intermediate-level feature fusion outperforms other fusion techniques, and it achieves the best performance with an overall binary accuracy of 74.0% on video+text modalities. Our work also improves feature selection for unimodal sentiment analysis, while proposing a novel and effective multimodal fusion architecture for this task.

1 Introduction

Sentiment analysis is the study on the underlying attitude that one holds towards a certain entity. For a long time, text-based sentiment analysis has been the staple in this area and only recently are other modalities being considered for sentiment analysis such as vision and speech (Poria et al., 2015). For text channels, the features usually include information about word sequences and meaning (Mikolov et al., 2013). However, combining information from multiple modalities can bring additional information to ambiguous

cases. For example, a smile extracted from facial features could help disambiguate cases such us "This movie is sick". Text alone would have trouble interpreting the meaning of the word "sick" in this context. This motivates the research of multimodal sentiment analysis. We seek to exploit the inter-dependencies between audio, text, and visual modalities in order to label video segments that exhibit positive or negative sentiment.

In current studies in this field, visual features often involve salient points of the face or body (Zadeh et al., 2016a), while low-level descriptors are collected from the speech signal such as pitch and volume (Zeng et al., 2009). The combination of features which have originated from text, speech and audio is what forms the basis of our multimodal classification work. Features from each modality are modeled, learned, and eventually *fused* together at various levels in a classification Deep Neural Network (DNN) system. When the modalities are fused together, this is called *multimodal fusion*. DNN multimodal fusion for binary sentiment classification is an active area of research that continues to gain momentum and spark interest due to the challenging nature of the problem (e.g., Poria et al. (2018)). We explore the interplay between three modalities: text, video, and audio. We focus on three fusion techniques inspired by previous work on multimodal fusion (Poria et al., 2018; Zadeh et al., 2016b).

We developed and compared three multimodal fusion architectures: (1) Input-level features fusion, (2) Intermediate features fusion, and (3) Decision-level fusion (late fusion). The first method refers to fusing information at the level of input features, similar to an unweighted concatenation of feature vectors, and it is the most widely used. The second method evokes the notion that each modality can be learned using a unimodal DNN. The weights learned through train-

Proceedings of the First Grand Challenge and Workshop on Human Multimodal Language (Challenge-HML), pages 64–72,
Melbourne, Australia July 20, 2018. ©2018 Association for Computational Linguistics

ing each unimodal DNN are concatenated together and training continues before the decision level. The third method, also known as *ensemble fusion* or *late fusion*, fuses multiple modalities at the decision level. We present our multimodal DNN fusion approaches in detail in our methodology description in Section 3. where we further analyze the interactions between modalities. We experimented with combinations of modalities as well as system architectures that attempt to capture the interplay between modalities.

2   Related Work

Sentiment analysis has traditionally been a task for natural language processing and based explicitly on text data, such as online blog posts (Feng et al., 2011). Beyond the scope of text-based sentiment analysis, Chen et al. (1998) provides us with an early work on audio-visual emotion recognition and showed that bimodal classifiers can perform better than unimodal ones alone.

Even though there is a significant amount of research done on audio-visual emotion recognition, only a few previous efforts have systematically explored trimodal fusion by combining text data with audio and visual modalities. Morency et al. (2011) was one of the first to investigate sentiment analysis on video movie reviews. They analyzed a collection of 47 videos depicting monologues in addition to the corresponding text that they manually transcribed from each 30-seconds excerpt. They evaluated sentiment for each review as a 3-way classification problem: positive, negative or neutral and achieved an F1 measure of 55.3%, which is much better than chance.

Furthermore, Wöllmer et al. (2013) attempted the same type of multimodal sentiment task for movie reviews using a linear Support Vector Machines (SVM) for the linguistic features and a Bidirectional Long Short-Term Memory (BLSTM) for the audiovisual ones. Our work continues this direction of combining data from different modalities and we also used video movie reviews. However, these related studies used very small collections of videos, whereas our work uses more than 2,000 videos.

Poria et al. (2015) provided a novel use of deep Convolutional Neural Networks (CNNs). They extracted features from the text modality and then adopted multiple kernel learning (MKL) for classifying the multimodal fused feature vectors. Most previous work has verified that multimodal classifiers perform better than unimodal ones.

More recently, Poria et al. (2018) presented three fusion techniques for multimodal sentiment analysis which achieved high accuracy: concatenation-based fusion, context-aware fusion and context-aware fusion with attention. One major issue of early fusion is that input-level feature concatenation will increase the feature space, which can be potentially problematic for very large datasets. To account for this, we experimented with principle components analysis (PCA) as a dimensionality reduction technique.

Existing top-performing systems on the CMU-MultimodalDataSDK MOSI (Zadeh et al., 2018) dataset are listed in Table 1, measured by classification accuracy. The state-of-the-art is Zadeh et al. (2017) which used tenor-based multimodal fusion. The C-MKL system of Poria et al. (2015), as discussed earlier, used a novel approach with CNNs. We also include a non-DNN system from Zadeh et al. (2016b) because it used input-level feature fusion, similar to one of our approaches in this work. Note that each of these systems has used slightly different feature selection techniques, which have introduced some inconsistencies between systems making a direct comparison difficult. Thus, we cannot make a direct system-to-system comparison between our methods and previous work.Additional work has been carried out on unimodal and multimodal sentiment analysis, using datasets different from CMU MOSI (Poria et al., 2016; Ma et al., 2018).

System	Authors	Acc
TFN	Zadeh et al. (2017)	77.1%
GME-LSTM(A)	Chen et al. (2017)	76.5%
C-MKL	Poria et al. (2015)	73.1%
SVM-MD	Zadeh et al. (2016b)	71.6%

Table 1: Accuracy reported in previous work on trimodal fusion for binary sentiment classification using MOSI dataset. Note that these systems differ slightly in terms of data pre-processing.

3   Methodology

Here we provide the technical specifications of the DNN architectures and parameters that we used in this work, followed by details about our three fusion techniques. We then discuss PCA dimensionality reduction, which we used in our experiments as a form of feature selection.

3.1 Data and Task Description

We conducted our experiments on the Multimodal Opinion level Sentiment Intensity (MOSI) dataset from CMU-MultimodalDataSDK (Zadeh et al., 2018).[1] The MOSI dataset is a collection of 2199 opinion video clips, each annotated with sentiment scores in the range [-3,3]: strongly positive (+3), positive (+2), weakly positive (+1), neutral (0), weakly negative (-1), negative (-2), strongly negative (-3). The multimodal observations consist of transcribed speech and features extracted from the visual and audio data. This benchmark dataset provided pre-extracted features on three modalities, a speaker-independent data partition of train (1283 items), validation (229 items), and test (686 items) sets, and an alignment of text, acoustic and visual data.

A detailed description of the dataset features and the sentiment class labels can be found in Zadeh et al. (2018). We aligned the features to the text embeddings as a reference and we max-normalized the feature values on a per-modality basis, as this allows for a meaningful comparison across systems. Due to the different number of timesteps in each utterance, we were required to restrict each sentence to a fixed size length by padding or cropping the sentences, using a maximum length. We treated this maximum length as a hyper-parameter and is described in more detail.

Primarily, our prediction task is binary classification for sentiment: positive versus negative. An exemplar with score $s > 0$ belongs to the positive class, while scores of $s < 0$ belong to the negative class. We transformed all scores to True/False values, where True corresponds to the positive class. For performance metrics, we used overall accuracy on the held-out test set.

After we identified the best-performing overall trimodal fusion system, we conducted additional experiments to report 5-class accuracy with F1 measure, as well as regression where we report mean-absolute error (MAE). These additional metrics allow further comparison of our best system to existing systems for this dataset.

3.2 Unimodal classifiers

We describe three types of DNNs that we used in our experiments for sentiment prediction and

---

[1]https://github.com/A2Zadeh/CMU-MultimodalDataSDK

some of the reasoning behind these selections.

Convolutional Neural Networks (CNNs) have been applied to various text-based sentiment and emotion detection tasks in natural language processing (Kim, 2014). Moreover, CNNs were used in OpenFace (Baltrušaitis et al., 2016), an open-source face recognition tool which was employed by MOSI. While there are limited studies that involve using CNNs to predict sentiment directly from speech, we note that others have successfully tested its efficacy by working directly on the speech spectrogram (Niu et al., 2017).

Long Short-Term Memory (LSTMs) are popular with sequence prediction tasks, because they can capture context from previous steps. LSTMs also achieved moderate success for video emotion detection Chen et al. (2017). We expect LSTMs to be useful in our sentiment prediction task due to the sequential nature of the video data.

Bidirectional LSTMs (BLSTMs) increase the amount of available contextual information by including both a forward pass and a backward pass through a sequence. There is growing interest in applying BLSTMs for emotion detection from visual and audio features (Ullah et al., 2018).

3.3 Training Hyper-parameters

The activation function we used across all of our experiments was ReLu (Nair and Hinton, 2010). The learning rule was Adam (Kingma and Ba, 2014) with standard parameters. For 1D convolution layers, the kernel size was 3. For max pooling layers, the window size was 2. We varied the number of convolutional layers in $[1, 2, 3]$. For LSTMs and Bi-directional LSTMs, we set the number of units to $[64]$ and the number of layers in $[1, 2, 3]$. For fully connected layers, we set the number of units to 100 and explored the number of layers in $[1, 2, 3]$. We added dropout (Srivastava et al., 2014) between fully connected layers with dropout rate in $[0.1, 0.2]$. In all experiments, we used early stopping with the stopping criteria set to identify maximum validation accuracy and patience was set to 10. We varied the maximum length setting for the video segments in our dataset, known as *maxlen*, in $[15, 20, 25, 30]$. The experiments employed batch normalization with batch size set to $b = 64$ (Ioffe and Szegedy, 2015). Since it is a binary classification task, we use a single output unit with sigmoid activation. The loss function we use is binary cross-entropy. We present test set results measuring overall accuracy.

3.4 Input-Level Feature Fusion

Input-level feature fusion (early fusion) refers to simply concatenating features from all the modalities, after they have been aligned and transformed to fixed size length. The concatenation is performed on the time step dimension. After input concatenation, the process follows a standard deep learning pipeline and we can apply different deep learning structures on top of the concatenated features. In this work, we tested CNNs, LSTMs and BLSTMs. We explored using one fully connected hidden layer and one output layer for the final prediction. In each case, we optimize the hyperparameters of the DNN as described earlier.

We experimented with dimensionality reduction on a per-modality basis, prior to feature concatenation. This is motivated by our observation that many of the visual and audio features were zero valued. Thus, we attempt to identify the most important features using PCA. Our system architecture for input-level fusion with and without dimensionality reduction is displayed in Figure 1.

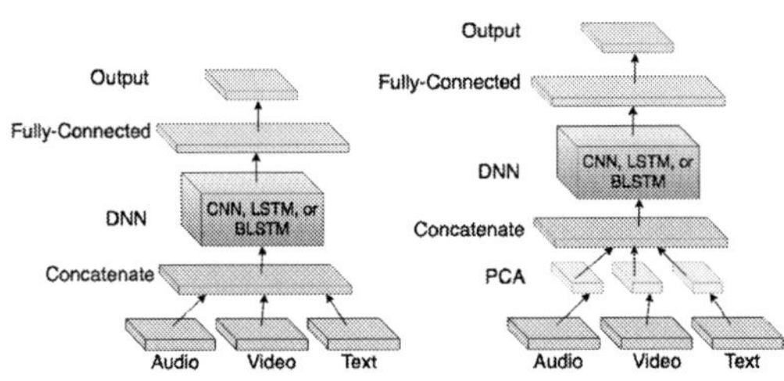

Figure 1: Input-level feature fusion architecture with and without PCA.

3.5 Intermediate-Level Feature Fusion

In intermediate-level feature fusion, data from each modality is first input to the best performing unimodal networks (for video and audio we use CNN, for text we use BLSTMs) which learn intermediate features. The intermediate weights from these unimodal networks are then concatenated and we then add fully connected layers to continue training the concatenated features. The goal is to capture interactions between modalities. We experimented with and without PCA on the input-level features. We show the architecture of the intermediate-level fusion system in Figure 2.

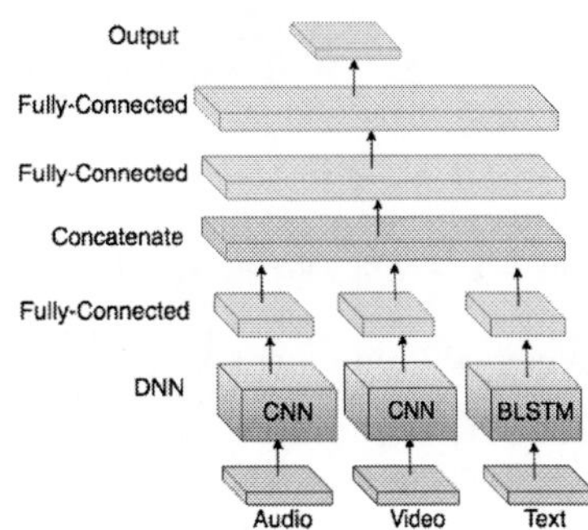

Figure 2: Intermediate-level feature fusion architecture. PCA for dimensionality reduction is not shown in this diagram.

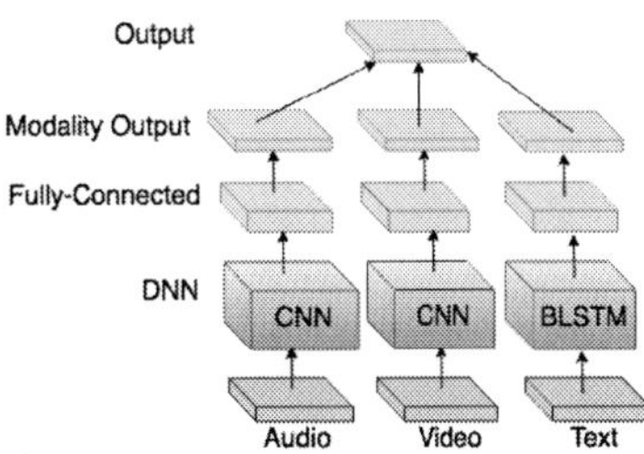

Figure 3: Late decision-level fusion architecture. PCA for dimensionality reduction is not shown in this diagram.

3.6 Decision-Level Feature Fusion

Decision-level feature fusion (late fusion) applies a separate classifier to weight the decisions of unimodal DNNs. The idea is that combining the unimodal results may improve model robustness. The most straightforward way of doing decision-level fusion is to train separate classifiers and weight their outputs with a tuple: $w = (\lambda_1, \lambda_2, \lambda_3)$. These weights can either be learned by another classifier, or set experimentally. No concatenation is performed in decision-level fusion. Compared to intermediate level fusion, which used sub-networks to extract intermediate features, here we output the decision of each modality.

Commonly, an SVM or another classifier is used on top of the decisions of each unimodal classifier. Our approach is different from existing literature in that we train 3 separate unimodal sub-networks such that our final system contains 3 component networks. For an illustration, refer to Figure 3. The top layer of this network is simply an output layer that receives the output of each modality sub-network (so the input is a one dimensional vector of size 3) and assigns a weight for each. This architecture acts as an ensemble of the 3 separate modality classifiers. Although it is not the case for our experiments, it would be possible to pre-train each modality on a different dataset, if more data is available (Wu et al., 1999).

3.7 Principal Component Analysis (PCA)

We applied PCA as a way to select the most valuable features, and reduce the dimensionality of the feature space, and ultimately to increase the unimodal performance. Our goal in using PCA was to find the most effective and least redundant components to the unimodal representation of the data since features are semantically different after they are max-normalized (Zadeh et al., 2017).

PCA is an important linear transformation technique for dimensionality reduction. PCA yields the ordered feature vectors, commonly referred to as *principal components*, which maximize the variance of the data by removing redundant features (Abdi and Williams, 2010). As a data reduction technique, PCA is commonly used for handling high-dimensional visual information in various research areas, such as medical images (Bhat et al., 2017), and has been proved to be an effective method for feature selection and extraction.

We used the Python Sklearn PCA decomposition function (Pedregosa et al., 2011) on our training set. We computed the proportion of variance explained by the number of principal components utilized using a scree plot.[2] We then inferred a range of k-components that might be responsible for a high enough cumulative variance and swept this range of k-component values (shown in Table 2). We applied the PCA fit that we learned from training data and used it as the PCA transform on our validation and test data. We continued with the unimodal classifier training according to the fusion architectures and hyper-parameters described earlier. We then examined binary test accuracy on each DNN architecture to determine the best value for k in PCA. The top-performing system is highlighted in bold.

4 Experiment Results

In this section we provide the experiments on the 3 fusion techniques with and without PCA, for predicting the positive/negative sentiment of the

---

[2]commonly employed when there is a need to assess which components explain the most variability in the data, plots available upon request

DNN	Mode	Test Acc(%)		k, Var
		-PCA	+PCA	
LSTM	A	54.0	55.2	10, 0.61
BLSTM	A	53.0	55.1	10, 0.61
CNN	**A**	**55.2**	**57.2**	**20, 0.82**
LSTM	V	54.2	56.7	25, 0.94
BLSTM	V	55.8	56.5	20, 0.90
CNN	**V**	**57.8**	**57.1**	**25, 0.94**
LSTM	**T**	**70.1**	**71.7**	**110, 0.98**
BLSTM	T	69.7	70.8	110, 0.98
CNN	T	67.7	68.5	130, 0.99

Table 2: Unimodal binary accuracy, exploring k number of PCA components with corresponding variance threshold (A=audio, V=video, T=text).

videos. We report accuracy for the binary sentiment classification problem. After experimenting with the fusion techniques, we identify the best overall performing systems and further report the 5-class accuracy, F1, and regression MAE and correlation.

4.1 Input-Level Feature Fusion

We explored input feature fusion with and without PCA. When we ran early fusion with PCA, we used the k-PCA components value described in Table 2. Our experiment results for early fusion are displayed in Table 3. The top-performing systems for each modality combination are highlighted in bold.

DNN	Mode	Test Acc(%)		Best
		-PCA	+PCA	Parameters
LSTM	A,V,T	70.5	70.1	1, 0.2, 25
BLSTM	**A,V,T**	**71.4**	**71.8**	**3, 0.2, 25**
CNN	A,V,T	69.2	68.5	1, 0.2, 20
LSTM	A,T	69.2	70.8	2, 0.2, 30
BLSTM	**A,T**	**71.2**	**71.2**	**1, 0.2, 25**
CNN	A,T	68.3	68.3	1, 0.1, 30
LSTM	V,T	72.3	69.5	2, 0.2, 30
BLSTM	**V,T**	**72.4**	**69.3**	**2, 0.2, 30**
CNN	V,T	69.3	68.8	3, 0.2, 30
LSTM	A,V	55.1	55.8	3, 0.1, 20
BLSTM	A,V	55.1	56.7	3, 0.1, 30
CNN	**A,V**	**55.6**	**57.4**	**2, 0.1, 30**

Table 3: Bimodal/trimodal binary accuracy for early fusion. Parameters refer to DNN layers, dropout rate, segment length.

The gains from PCA for input-level fusion are particularly small, which is counter-intuitive considering that early fusion concatenation increases the dimensionality of the data. The best-performing overall system was a BLSTM using bimodal text and video data at 72.4% binary accuracy without PCA. The CNN tends to perform less well across all bimodal/trimodal combinations, and this suggests that emotion prediction has a sequential aspect. That sequential aspect is picked up by the other DNNs that we tested.

4.2 Intermediate-Level Feature Fusion

The intermediate features fusion model we proposed adds dense layers on top of the intermediate weights extracted from each modality. There are other possible configurations to be explored, but we experimented with the simplest one. Compared to early fusion, the features for each modality are first fed to a different network. We have chosen the best performing network for each single modality as described in Table 2 (CNN for audio and video, and BLSTM for text) for the pre-fusion stages.

Mode	Test Acc(%)		Best
	-PCA	+PCA	Params
A,V,T	73.3	73.0	1, 0.1, 30
A,V	60.0	59.0	3, 0.1, 30
A,T	70.5	70.8	2, 0.2, 25
V,T	**74.0**	**74.0**	**3, 0.2, 30**

Table 4: Bimodal/trimodal binary accuracy for intermediate feature fusion. Parameters refer to DNN layers, dropout rate, segment length.

When we applied PCA for intermediate-level fusion, we applied it either to all modalities or none. This configuration makes it possible to make a direct comparison with our other approaches. Results are summarized in Table 4. We achieve our highest performance so far which was the bimodal fusion of video and text with binary accuracy of 74.0%. We note that this accuracy was achieved with and without PCA, suggesting either that our proposed system is robust to noise or that video and text data was not particularly noisy.

4.3 Decision-Level Fusion

For our decision-level fusion (late fusion) experiments, we kept the pre-fusion network consistent with intermediate fusion (CNN for audio and video, BLSTM for text). Experiment results are in Table 5. Our best result is for the trimodal inputs. We find that the results are not much different from a carefully trained text only predictor. Since the video and audio classifiers are much worse predictors than text. This indicates that a decision level classifier is not the best approach for the MOSI dataset. We noticed that the top-performing decision-level systems used less segment length context than our previous experiments, even though the performance is comparable. This could be due to the fact that the combination of modalities creates a form of information enhancement, so that less context is needed to make a prediction.

Mode	Test Acc(%)		Best
	-PCA	+PCA	Params
A,V,T	70.6	70.8	2, 0.1, 25
A,V	56.8	58.1	1, 0.2, 25
A,T	71.7	71.7	3, 0.1, 15
V,T	**72.5**	**72.0**	**1, 0.1, 30**

Table 5: Bimodal/trimodal binary accuracy for decision-level fusion experiments.

4.4 Detailed Top Performing Systems

To make a comparison to performance reported in previous work, we provide more specific performance metrics in Table 6, based on the top-performing systems from each of the 3 fusion methods that we have discussed. For each top system, we report the binary accuracy and $F1$ score, the 5-class accuracy, and the regression MAE and Pearson r correlation (values closer to $r = 1$ indicate positive correlation, while values closer to $r = -1$ indicate negative correlation).

All of our best-performing systems used bimodal (text+video) feature fusion instead of trimodal. Across all systems, we can generalize that leaving out the audio modality improved performance. Our top input-level fusion system ($Early$) was bimodal BLSTM without PCA. Our top intermediate-level fusion system ($Inter.$), was bimodal fusion regardless of PCA. Finally, our best decision-level system ($Late$) was bimodal without PCA.

5 Discussion and Analysis

Our unimodal experiments showed that applying PCA always yields improved performance for bi-

Top	Binary		5-class	Regress.	
Method	Acc	F1	Acc	MAE	r
Early	72.4	66.7	33.3	1.08	0.55
Inter.	**74.0**	**65.6**	**35.2**	**1.10**	**0.56**
Late	72.5	66.3	31.4	1.05	0.56

Table 6: Top fusion system performance on binary classification, 5-class classification and regression.

nary sentiment prediction on this dataset. Further, we were able to identify text as the single best-performing and audio as the worst-performing modality predictor. Although PCA improved unimodal performance, it did not have an effect on the intermediate and decision fusions. This could be due to inherent noise in the audio data from the CMU-MultimodalDataSDK, which our feature selection procedure did not remedy.

We present example negative and positive sentences in Table 7 and the scores given by our best performing classifier. A score above 0.5 classifies the sentences as positive. This outlines the difficulty of the task and shows that some sentences are difficult to label even for humans.

Sentence text	Truth	Score
The voice acting was phenomenal	+	0.94
It was like this like pouty like grumpy look	-	0.31
Now the real Steven Russel has like an IQ like 163 which is like wow genius	**+**	**0.49**
If you know they're in there this is a cheesy um movie	**-**	**0.80**

Table 7: Example sentences and their true labels. Incorrect classification is distinguished in bold/red.

6 Conclusions and Future Work

Despite our efforts to reduce feature redundancy during early fusion, we found an apparent ceiling in terms of the best binary accuracy, as it never reached above 74.0%. Our experiments showed that PCA improves test accuracy in the case of unimodal models and sometimes the early fusion model. Interestingly, in our bimodal and trimodal experiments, we found that leaving out audio and

focusing on video+text features, always yields a slight improvement. This is consistent with the state of the art on the MOSI dataset (Zadeh et al., 2017) which found that audio is the weakest of all three modalities for this dataset. It would be interesting to disentangle whether or not this constitutes bias in the data or bias in human communication or perception of emotions.

As the goal of our study was to explore multimodal fusion techniques, we explored 3 different fusion architectures that all yield better results that unimodal classifiers. This indicates that there are interactions to be learned during the fusion process. We showed that both late decision-level fusion and early fusion can achieve comparable results. As a task for future work, we encourage exploring the best intervention point for intermediate-level fusion. For example, to vary the number of fully-connected layers on individual DNNs before concatenation. Similarly, it should be investigated how to weigh the DNNs before concatenation as we know that text is often the best unimodal predictor of sentiment.

In terms of combining the CNN architecture with PCA, CNNs will basically learn common structural components across the input features, which can be viewed as a redundancy that is removed by PCA. Therefore this combination would only useful to the extent that it helps with removing actual noise from the data. Similarly, this combination of CNN+PCA on audio-only data, which consists primarily of MFCC's, also creates a type of redundancy. Given that there could be better models than PCA, we encourage future work to systematically explore and compare techniques for both feature selection and noise reduction on the CMU MOSI dataset.

In the future, we plan to examine which of the low-level acoustic descriptors, facial features, and words are the most effective for sentiment analysis. This would help future studies to learn better feature representations for sentiment analysis. Further, we selected our top-performing models based on binary classification accuracy, without a category for "neutral". It could be the case that some of our data exemplars were a better fit for this third category, or that audio features are predictive of a neutral category, something that should be investigated in future work.

The MOSI dataset breaks down each movie review into sentences to be classified individually, losing context that might be gained by looking at the other neighboring sentences. Motivated by Poria et al. (2017) who suggested contextual sentiment analysis, we plan on including additional contextual information when predicting the sentiment of a sentence. Instead of considering each utterance as a separate entity, we will add contextual information from neighboring sentences belonging to the same monologue and study the gain.

Acknowledgments

This work was supported in part by the EPSRC Centre for Doctoral Training in Data Science, funded by the UK Engineering and Physical Sciences Research Council (grant EP/L016427/1) and the University of Edinburgh. The authors would like to thank Steve Renals at University of Edinburgh Centre for Speech Technology Research (CSTR) and the anonymous reviewers for their valuable comments.

References

Hervé Abdi and Lynne J Williams. 2010. Principal Component Analysis. *Wiley Interdisciplinary Reviews: Computational Statistics*, 2(4):433–459.

Tadas Baltrušaitis, Peter Robinson, and Louis-Philippe Morency. 2016. Openface: An Open Source Facial Behavior Analysis Toolkit. In *IEEE Winter Conference on Applications of Computer Vision*.

Mahima Bhat, Maya V Karki, et al. 2017. Feature Selection Based on PCA and PSO for Multimodal Medical Image Fusion Using DTCWT. *arXiv preprint arXiv:1701.08918*.

Lawrence S. Chen, Huang Thomas S., Tsutomu Miyasato, and Ryohei Nakatsu. 1998. Multimodal Human emotion/expression recognition. In *Proceedings Third IEEE International Conference on Automatic Face and Gesture Recognition*, pages 366–371.

Minghai Chen, Sen Wang, Paul Pu Liang, Tadas Baltrušaitis, Amir Zadeh, and Louis-Philippe Morency. 2017. Multimodal Sentiment Analysis With Word-Level Fusion and Reinforcement Learning. In *Proceedings of the 19th ACM International Conference on Multimodal Interaction*, pages 163–171. ACM.

Shi Feng, Daling Wang, Ge Yu, Wei Gao, and Kam-Fai Wong. 2011. Extracting Common Emotions From Blogs Based on Fine-Grained Sentiment Clustering. *Knowledge and Information Systems*, 27(2):281–302.

Sergey Ioffe and Christian Szegedy. 2015. Batch Normalization: Accelerating Deep Network Training by Reducing Internal Covariate Shift. In *International Conference on Machine Learning*, pages 448–456.

Yoon Kim. 2014. Convolutional Neural Networks for Sentence Classification. *CoRR*, abs/1408.5882.

Diederik Kingma and Jimmy Ba. 2014. Adam: A Method for Stochastic Optimization. *arXiv preprint arXiv:1412.6980*.

Yukun Ma, Haiyun Peng, Tahir Khan, Erik Cambria, and Amir Hussain. 2018. Sentic LSTM: A Hybrid Network for Targeted Aspect-Based Sentiment Analysis. *Cognitive Computation*, pages 1–12.

Tomas Mikolov, Kai Chen, Greg Corrado, and Jeffrey Dean. 2013. Efficient Estimation of Word Representations in Vector Space. *CoRR*, abs/1301.3781.

Louis-Philippe Morency, Rada Mihalcea, and Payal Doshi. 2011. Towards Multimodal Sentiment Analysis: Harvesting Opinions from the Web. In *Proceedings of the 13th International Conference on Multimodal Interfaces*, ICMI '11, pages 169–176, New York, NY, USA. ACM.

Vinod Nair and Geoffrey E. Hinton. 2010. Rectified Linear Units Improve Restricted Boltzmann Machines. In *Proceedings of the 27th International Conference on International Conference on Machine Learning*, ICML'10, pages 807–814, USA.

Yafeng Niu, Dongsheng Zou, Yadong Niu, Zhongshi He, and Hua Tan. 2017. A Breakthrough in Speech Emotion Recognition Using Deep Retinal Convolution Neural Networks. *arXiv preprint arXiv:1707.09917*.

Fabian Pedregosa, Gaël Varoquaux, Alexandre Gramfort, Vincent Michel, Bertrand Thirion, Olivier Grisel, Mathieu Blondel, Peter Prettenhofer, Ron Weiss, Vincent Dubourg, et al. 2011. Scikit-Learn: Machine Learning in Python. *Journal of Machine Learning Research*, 12(Oct):2825–2830.

Soujanya Poria, Erik Cambria, and Alexander Gelbukh. 2015. Deep Convolutional Neural Network Textual Features and Multiple Kernel Learning for Utterance-Level Multimodal Sentiment Analysis. In *Proceedings Empirical Methods in Natural Language Processing (EMNLP)*, pages 2539–2544.

Soujanya Poria, Erik Cambria, Devamanyu Hazarika, Navonil Majumder, Amir Zadeh, and Louis-Philippe Morency. 2017. Context-Dependent Sentiment Analysis in User-Generated Videos. In *Proceedings of the 55th Annual Meeting of the Association for Computational Linguistics (Volume 1: Long Papers)*, volume 1, pages 873–883.

Soujanya Poria, Iti Chaturvedi, Erik Cambria, and Amir Hussain. 2016. Convolutional MKL Based Multimodal Emotion Recognition and Sentiment Analysis. In *Data Mining (ICDM), 2016 IEEE 16th International Conference on*, pages 439–448. IEEE.

Soujanya Poria, Navonil Majumder, Devamanyu Hazarika, Erik Cambria, Amir Hussain, and Alexander Gelbukh. 2018. Multimodal Sentiment Analysis: Addressing Key Issues and Setting up Baselines. *ArXiv e-prints*.

Nitish Srivastava, Geoffrey Hinton, Alex Krizhevsky, Ilya Sutskever, and Ruslan Salakhutdinov. 2014. Dropout: A Simple Way to Prevent Neural Networks From Overfitting. *Journal of Machine Learning Research*, 15:1929–1958.

Amin Ullah, Jamil Ahmad, Khan Muhammad, Muhammad Sajjad, and Sung Wook Baik. 2018. Action Recognition in Video Sequences Using Deep Bi-Directional LSTM With CNN Features. *IEEE Access*, 6:1155–1166.

Martin Wöllmer, Felix Weninger, Tobias Knaup, Björn Schuller, Congkai Sun, Kenji Sagae, and Louis-Philippe Morency. 2013. Youtube Movie Reviews: Sentiment Analysis in an Audio-Visual Context. *IEEE Intelligent Systems*, 28(3):46–53.

Lizhong Wu, S. L. Oviatt, and P. R. Cohen. 1999. Multimodal Integration - A Statistical View. *IEEE Transactions on Multimedia*, 1(4):334–341.

Amir Zadeh, Minghai Chen, Soujanya Poria, Erik Cambria, and Louis-Philippe Morency. 2017. Tensor Fusion Network for Multimodal Sentiment Analysis. *CoRR*, abs/1707.07250.

Amir Zadeh, Paul Pu Liang, Soujanya Poria, Prateek Vij, Erik Cambria, and Louis-Philippe Morency. 2018. Multi-Attention Recurrent Network for Human Communication Comprehension. In *arXiv preprint arXiv:1802.00923*.

Amir Zadeh, Rowan Zellers, Eli Pincus, and Louis-Philippe Morency. 2016a. MOSI: Multimodal Corpus of Sentiment Intensity and Subjectivity Analysis in Online Opinion Videos. *CoRR*, abs/1606.06259.

Amir Zadeh, Rowan Zellers, Eli Pincus, and Louis-Philippe Morency. 2016b. Multimodal Sentiment Intensity Analysis in Videos: Facial Gestures and Verbal Messages. *IEEE Intelligent Systems*, 31(6):82–88.

Zhihong Zeng, Maja Pantic, Glenn I Roisman, and Thomas S Huang. 2009. A Survey of Affect Recognition Methods: Audio, Visual, and Spontaneous Expressions. *IEEE Transactions on Pattern Analysis and Machine Intelligence*, 31(1):39–58.

Author Index